Language and Thought

This book fulfils the need for a clear overview of this area of cognitive psychology which encompasses both language and thought. Focusing on goal-directed thinking and decision-making, Nick Lund looks at the relationship between our grasp of language and our problem-solving abilities. Different positions on the issues are contextualised and discussed in a way suitable for the AQA-A A-level syllabus. Supplementary detail means that the book will also be valuable to other A-level specification candidates and undergraduates coming to this area for the first time.

Nick Lund is Senior Lecturer in Psychology at Manchester Metropolitan University and is author of *Animal Cognition* and *Attention and Pattern Recognition* in the Routledge Modular Psychology series.

Routledge Modular Psychology

Series editors: Cara Flanagan is a Reviser for AS and A2 level Psychology and an experienced teacher and examiner. Philip Banyard is Associate Senior Lecturer in Psychology at Nottingham Trent University and a Chief Examiner for AS and A2 level Psychology.

The *Routledge Modular Psychology* series is a completely new approach to introductory-level psychology, tailor-made to the new modular style of teaching. Each short book covers a topic in more detail than any large textbook can, allowing teacher and student to select material exactly to suit any particular course or project.

The books have been written especially for those students new to higher-level study, whether at school, college or university. They include specially designed features to help with technique, such as a model essay at an average level with an examiner's comments to show how extra marks can be gained. The authors are all examiners and teachers at the introductory level.

The *Routledge Modular Psychology* texts are all user-friendly and accessible and include the following features:

- practice essays with specialist commentary to show how to achieve a higher grade
- chapter summaries to assist with revision
- progress and review exercises
- glossary of key terms
- summaries of key research
- further reading to stimulate ongoing study and research
- cross-referencing to other books in the series

For more details on our AS, A2 and *Routledge Modular Psychology* publications visit our website at www.a-levelpsychology.co.uk

Also available in this series (titles listed by syllabus section):

ATYPICAL DEVELOPMENT AND ABNORMAL BEHAVIOUR

Psychopathology
John D. Stirling and Jonathan S.E. Hellewell

Therapeutic Approaches in Psychology
Susan Cave

Classification and Diagnosis of Abnormal Psychology
Susan Cave

BIO-PSYCHOLOGY

Cortical Functions
John Stirling

The Physiological Basis of Behaviour: Neural and hormonal processes
Kevin Silber

Awareness: Biorhythms, sleep and dreaming
Evie Bentley

COGNITIVE PSYCHOLOGY

Memory and Forgetting
John Henderson

Perception: Theory, development and organisation
Paul Rookes and Jane Willson

Attention and Pattern Recognition
Nick Lund

DEVELOPMENTAL PSYCHOLOGY

Early Socialisation: Sociability and attachment
Cara Flanagan

Social and Personality Development
Tina Abbott

PERSPECTIVES AND RESEARCH

Controversies in Psychology
Philip Banyard

Ethical Issues and Guidelines in Psychology
Cara Flanagan and Philip Banyard (forthcoming)

Introducing Research and Data in Psychology: A guide to methods and analysis
Ann Searle

Theoretical Approaches in Psychology
Matt Jarvis

Debates in Psychology
Andy Bell

SOCIAL PSYCHOLOGY

Social Influences
Kevin Wren

Interpersonal Relationships
Diana Dwyer

Social Cognition
Donald C. Pennington

COMPARATIVE PSYCHOLOGY

Determinants of Animal Behaviour
JoAnne Cartwright

Evolutionary Explanations of Human Behaviour
John Cartwright

Animal Cognition
Nick Lund

OTHER TITLES

Sport Psychology
Matt Jarvis

Health Psychology
Anthony Curtis

Psychology and Work
Christine Hodson

Psychology and Education
Susan Bentham

Psychology and Crime
David Putwain and Aidan Sammons

STUDY GUIDE

Exam Success in AQA(A) Psychology
Paul Humphreys (forthcoming)

Language and Thought

Nick Lund

Routledge
Taylor & Francis Group

LONDON AND NEW YORK

First published 2003
by Routledge
27 Church Road, Hove, East Sussex BN3 2FA

Simultaneously published in the USA and Canada
by Routledge
29 West 35th Street, New York, NY10001

Routledge is an imprint of the Taylor & Francis Group

Typeset in Times and Frutiger by Keystroke,
Jacaranda Lodge, Wolverhampton
Printed and bound in Great Britain by
TJ International Ltd, Padstow, Cornwall

British Library Cataloguing in Publication Data
A catalogue record for this book is available from the British Library

Library of Congress Cataloging-in-Publication Data
Lund, Nick, 1956–
    Language and thought / Nick Lund.
        p. cm. — (Routledge modular psychology)
    Includes bibliographical references and index.
    ISBN 0–415–28292–6 (hardcover) —ISBN 0–415–28291–8 (pbk.)
1. Language and languages. 2. Thought and thinking.
3. Language acquisition. I. Title. II. Series.
P107 .L86 2003
410—dc21   2003000227

ISBN 0–415–28292–6 (hbk)
ISBN 0–415–28291–8 (pbk)

Contents

List of figures   xi

1 Introduction   1
Language and thought 1
The nature of language 2
Methods of studying language 3
Problem-solving and decision-making 4
The study of problem-solving and decision-making 5
Summary 7

2 The relationship between language and thought   9
Introduction 9
The linguistic relativity hypothesis 10
Thought determines language 22
The interdependence of language and thought 24
Summary 26
Review exercise 27

3 Social and cultural aspects of language   29
Introduction 29
Social class 30
Ethnic background 32
Gender 33

Summary 36
Review exercise 37

4 Language acquisition 39
Introduction 39
The stages of language acquisition 40
Pre-linguistic stage 40
One-word stage 41
Development of grammar 43
Meaning and pragmatics 46
Summary 48
Review exercise 49

5 Theories of language acquisition 51
Introduction 51
Environmental theories of language acquisition 52
Nativist theories of language acquisition 57
Social interactionist theories of language acquisition 61
Summary 62
Review exercise 63

6 Problem-solving 65
Introduction 65
Types of problems 66
Gestalt approach 69
Information-processing approach 73
Information processing and 'insight' 76
Use of analogy in problem-solving 77
Problem-solving in everyday life 81
Summary 82
Review exercise 83

7 Decision-making 85
Introduction 85
The heuristics and biases approach to judgements 86
Other factors that influence judgements 92
Evaluation of the heuristics and biases approach 95
Theories of decision-making 97

Summary   101
Review exercise 102

8 Study Aids   **103**
Improving your essay-writing skills   103
Practice essay 1   104
Practice essay 2   107
Key Research Summaries   110
Article 1 – Hunt & Agnoli (1991)   110
Article 2 – Saxton (1997)   112
Articles 3 and 4 – Kahneman & Tversky (1996)   114
                        Gigerenzer (1994)   114

Glossary   119
Solutions to problems   123
Bibliography   129
Index   139

Figures

2.1 The effect of labels on the subsequent redrawing of
    pictures   15
2.2 The hierarchy of the eleven basic colour terms   17
4.1 An experiment to test whether children use rules of
    grammar   45
6.1 The nine-dot problem   68
6.2 Tower of Hanoi   72
6.3 The Hobbits and Orcs problem   73

    Solution to the nine-dot problem (Figure 6.1)   123
    Solution to the Hobbits and Orcs problem (Figure 6.3)   124

1

Introduction

Language and thought
The nature of language
Methods of studying language
Problem-solving and decision-making
The study of problem-solving and decision-making
Summary

Language and thought

This book, *Language and Thought,* is one of the Routledge Modular Psychology series that deals with cognitive psychology. There are many ways of describing cognitive psychology, but Solso (1998) defines it as 'the scientific study of the thinking mind' (p.2). Cognitive psychology therefore covers a wide variety of areas of research including perception, attention, memory, language and thought. Language and thought are central to all human activities since they are the medium of our mental and social lives. Language is used both to communicate with others and to monitor our internal thoughts, or, as Harley (2001, p.1) notes, 'in some form or another it so dominates our social and cognitive activity that it would be difficult to imagine what life would be without it'. Many people regard the ability to use language and rational thought as uniquely human qualities and believe it is these abilities that distinguish humans from other animals. For example Harley (2001, p.1) considers language to be 'an essential part of what it means to be human, and it is partly what sets us apart from other animals'. Similarly Garnham and Oakhill (1994, p.16) suggest 'the nature and complexity of our thought processes . . . appear to set people apart from other animals'. This book is therefore concerned with topics that lie at the heart of cognitive psychology and, possibly, humanity.

The nature of language

Human language is a complex skill that defies a simple definition. In addition it can take many forms and can be spoken, written or signed. One way to encompass the complexity of language is to identify a range of characteristics that describe its essential features. For example, Hockett (1960) described sixteen 'design character-istics' which he believed were essential for human language. Some of the more important characteristics are displacement, arbitrariness, semanticity and productivity:

- Displacement is the ability to use language to discuss things removed in space and time (for example, you could talk of events that happened yesterday in Denmark).
- Arbitrariness refers to the symbolic nature of language; the sounds, symbols or signs we use to represent ideas or objects are arbitrary (for example, the word 'dog' does not sound like a dog or look like a dog when written, it just represents a dog).
- Semanticity is the meaning we assign these arbitrary symbols. Words have shared meaning that communicates ideas between people.
- Productivity describes the creativity of language. We can create and understand a vast number of novel sentences because we can combine and recombine words using rules. Even a bizarre sequence of words that we have not heard before can be under-stood if they are presented as a sentence. The phrase 'The aardvark bent the melon slowly' is odd, but if I ask you what the aardvark did you could answer!

There are a number of components to language, each of which is a field of study in itself. For example, phonology is the study of the sounds made in speech and the way these sounds are combined together. Morphology is concerned with the structure of words since words are made up of one or more smaller units called morphemes. Semantics is the study of the meaning of words or combination of words. Syntax, on the other hand, refers to the rules of how words and phrases can be combined together. It is the rules of syntax that govern whether word combinations are grammatical or not. Finally, pragmatics is the study of the use of language to communicate. There is more to a conversation than sharing common semantics and syntax because conversation requires turn-taking, being responsive to another person, etc. Pragmatics looks at the use of language in social interaction. Different theories of language acquisition tend to focus on different components of language, with some concentrating on syntax and others on pragmatics (see Chapter 5, p.61).

Language affects much of our lives and covers a wide variety of topic areas, such as speech, reading, writing, etc.; and it is beyond the scope of this book to study every aspect of language. This book will focus on certain aspects of language and, as language and thinking seem so interdependent, one focus is the relationship between language and thought (Chapter 2). Since language seems to have some influence on our perception of others another focus will be the social and cultural aspects of language (Chapter 3). A final focus will be on the development of language, starting with studies of the process of language acquisition (Chapter 4) before discussing the theories of language acquisition (Chapter 5).

Methods of studying language

The complexity of language has led to a wide range of methods being used to study it. The study of the relationship between language and thought has often been examined using cross-cultural studies of languages. These studies look both at differences in grammar between languages and at the number of words used to refer to objects/ situations in different cultures/countries. However, these studies can be problematic since it is not possible to do direct translations from one language to another (see p.13). Another approach is to look at the type of language children use at different stages of cognitive development to try to establish whether cognitive and linguistic development are linked. Social and cultural aspects of language also involve comparisons between groups. These comparisons can be used to investigate whether linguistic differences between groups affect thinking.

The development of language is studied in two main ways – either natural observation or more formal structured testing (Owens, 2001). Natural observation involves collecting examples of children's speech in natural settings such as home or school. This data can be collected in a variety of ways (audiotaping, videotaping, parental diaries, etc.) and can be unstructured (where the researcher simply records conversations with the child) or more structured (where the researcher tries to elicit speech about a topic). The obvious advantage of natural observation is that it provides a picture of a child's normal speech that might not be heard in a more formal study. However, although this method may provide a general picture of speech production, it may miss language that is infrequent. In addition the behaviour of the child may not reflect linguistic competence (Owens, 2001). More formal techniques such as structured testing or experiments allow researchers to collect information that may not be accessible from natural observation. For example, it is difficult to assess a child's comprehension of language from natural observation but it is relatively easy using structured tests. Tests also enable researchers to study forms of speech that do not occur often (e.g. passive sentences, see p.46). However, these techniques do not show how the child uses language in everyday use and may reflect the child's use of language in tests rather than normal language. Another measure used in the study of language development is the mean length of utterance or MLU. This is a measure of the average number of words in a sentence that a child uses and is normally calculated by counting the number of words used in 100 sentences and dividing by 100. The MLU is one measure of the complexity of children's speech. It is important to note that children's understanding of language, or comprehension, is not necessarily reflected in their speech (production). In the early stages of language acquisition comprehension typically precedes production.

Problem-solving and decision-making

Thinking is a complex process that affects every aspect of our lives and yet is something we take for granted. The term 'thinking' covers a wide range of activities and is difficult to define, but Solso (1998, p.420) defines it as 'a process by which a new mental representation is formed through the transformation of information by complex interaction of the mental attributes of judging, abstracting, reasoning, imaging, and problem solving'. He notes that there are three basic ideas about thinking. Firstly, thinking is cognitive; in other words, thinking involves an internal processing of information. Secondly, thinking involves manipulation of knowledge. Lastly, thinking is directed towards solutions. However, Eysenck and Keane (2000) suggest that thinking can vary in the extent in which it is directed from relatively undirected (e.g. 'daydreaming') to directed (e.g. solving a mathematical equation). This book is largely confined to the thought processes involved in goal-directed thinking or the type of thought involved in problem-solving and decision-making.

Problem-solving is a common feature of nearly every aspect of our lives. Problems occur at work, in social interactions, etc. A problem occurs when we have a goal but do not know how to reach it. For example, you might want to contact a friend who has lost their mobile phone. Here there is a clear goal but not a clear way of achieving it. Problem-solving is covered in Chapter 6. Decision-making is concerned with judgements and involves assessing then choosing from a number of alternatives. For example, you may have to decide whether to take a short holiday in an expensive location or a long holiday in a cheaper location. Decision-making is covered in Chapter 7. Eysenck and Keane (2000) point out that the division between problem-solving and decision-making reflects the way research about thinking has developed historically and is unlikely to be reflected in everyday thoughts (since often the decisions we make are about problems in our lives). However, the division does serve as a useful distinction to study the subject matter.

The study of problem-solving and decision-making

On one level the study of problem-solving and decision-making is relatively straightforward. Researchers can manipulate variables such as the instructions given, the type of problem, etc. and record the participants' responses such as the speed of problem-solving (Robertson, 2001). However, most researchers are interested in what happens between the presentation of the problem and the answer. In other words they are interested in the thought processes that led to the answer, and this can only be *inferred* from studying behaviour. The question of how to study mental activity, such as problem-solving and decision-making, has troubled psychologists throughout the history of psychology and has been at the heart of disputes about the subject matter of psychology. Early psychology was largely the study of mental life and involved introspective methods. In other words it involved participants trying to describe their own thoughts. This changed with the emergence of behaviourism when the emphasis was on the study of behaviour and any study of mental activity was viewed as unscientific (because it cannot be observed). With the rise of cognitive psychology there was renewed interest in mental activity. Cognitive psychology is concerned with how mental activity mediates behaviour. As noted earlier, Solso (1998, p.2) defines cognitive psychology as 'the scientific study of the thinking mind'. However, this raises a problem: how can something which cannot be observed be studied scientifically?

Garnham and Oakhill (1994) describe two main methods of studying the thought processes involved in problem-solving and decision-making: protocol analysis and computer modelling. **Protocol analysis** involves asking participants to 'think aloud' as they solve problems or make decisions. These verbal reports, or protocols, can then be analysed to gain information about the processes involved. A central assumption of the cognitive approach is that humans, like computers, have to process information. Much of this processing of information is not accessible because we are not aware of it. However, the results of these processes are available and form the words and images of our working memory and it is this that protocol analysis reveals (Robertson, 2001). A second method of studying the processes involved in problem-solving and decision-making is to use computer modelling. These are computer programs that are designed to simulate human problem-solving. This is also based on the information processing approach and the idea that problems are solved and decisions are made in a series of stages. Computer models are designed to simulate the process at each of these stages and if they can do so successfully then it is argued that it is likely that people use a similar sequence of processes.

Summary

Language and thought are central to the study of cognitive psychology and, some would argue, are defining aspects of humanity. Language is a complex skill that allows people to communicate an enormous number of messages using arbitrary symbols. People can use language to discuss things that are not present either in space or time. Language can be studied on many levels, including the sounds (phonology), the structure of words (morphology), the meaning of words (semantics), the rules for combining words (syntax) and the way language is used in a social setting (pragmatics). Language is studied in a variety of ways, depending on the emphasis of the research, and includes cross-cultural studies, naturalistic observation and structured testing. Problem-solving and decision-making are two important features of thinking. Problems occur when a person does not see how to achieve a goal state. Decision-making involves making judgements about alternatives and choosing one of them. Problem-solving and decision-making can be studied by manipulating the information given to participants and measuring various features of their responses. The cognitive processes underlying the problem-solving and decision-making are investigated using protocol analysis and computer modelling. Protocol analysis involves examining the verbal reports of participants while they are engaged in tasks to gain an insight into the underlying processes. Computer modelling is the use of computer programs to simulate human problem-solving and decision-making. These are used to investigate the nature and sequence of the processes involved.

Further reading

Garnham, A. and Oakhill, J. (1994) *Thinking and Reasoning*. Oxford: Blackwell. This is an advanced book which has excellent chapters on language and thought, problem-solving and decision-making.

Harley, T.A. (2001) *The Psychology of Language: From data to theory* (2nd edn). Hove: Psychology Press. This book is another advanced text but it covers all aspects of language in a clear and interesting fashion.

2

The relationship between language and thought

Introduction
The linguistic relativity hypothesis
Thought determines language
The interdependence of language and thought
Summary
Review exercise

Introduction

One feature that sets human communities apart from animal communities is the use of language. Language is a vital part of every human culture and is a powerful social tool that we master at an early age. A second feature of humans is our ability to solve complex and/or abstract problems. Although some animals are capable of solving simple problems none are capable of solving the problems involved in something like space exploration or even in the designing of a psychology experiment. For centuries philosophers have questioned whether these two abilities are related and, if so, what the nature of the relationship between language and thought is. At the beginning of the last century psychologists joined this debate and it is a topic that is currently generating a lot of research.

Another factor in the study of language and thought is the role of culture. When we study a language from another country we realise that it is not just the words and grammar that are different but the customs and traditions as well. Even the ideas of that culture and the way of dealing with life can be different. If people speaking different languages have different customs and ideas it raises the following question: do different languages lead to different ways of thinking?

Although there is some debate about the extent of language in thinking (see, for example, Carruthers, 1996), as adults much of our thinking seems to involve words and language. Furthermore, we cannot use language without thinking about what we want to say. Thus, in adults at least, language and thought seem closely entwined. There are four main views about the nature of this relationship between language and thought:

1. The language we speak determines or influences the way we think.
2. The way we think determines the use of language.
3. Language and thought are independent but gradually become interdependent during infancy.
4. Language and thought are independent.

The first of these views has been labelled the linguistic relativity hypothesis and is largely associated with Whorf; the second represents a view held by Piaget; the third by Vygotsky. These three views on the relationship between language and thought are discussed in this chapter. The fourth view has been proposed by Chomsky and is discussed in Chapter 5.

The linguistic relativity hypothesis

The **linguistic relativity hypothesis (LRH)** proposes that language influences the way people perceive and think about the world. This hypothesis concentrates on the differences in both vocabulary and grammar between different languages and suggests that speakers of a particular language are led to think, perceive and remember the world in a way peculiar to that language. Users of different languages will therefore tend to view the world differently. The theory is often traced back to the work of the linguist Sapir (1929) who compared English to a number of Native American languages. He concluded that the differences between the languages changed the way people perceive their environments. However, the LRH has become most closely associated with the work of Whorf (1956). He was another linguist who studied Native American languages and he became convinced that the differences between languages *determined* the types of thought people were able to have. The theory is often referred to as the Sapir– Whorf hypothesis or, because of the greater influence of Whorf's ideas, the **Whorfian hypothesis**.

Psychologists have recognised that there are at least two versions of the LRH which differ in emphasis and implications. These two versions of the hypothesis have been labelled 'strong' and 'weak':

- The 'strong' version is that language *determines* thought.
- The 'weak' version is that language *influences* thought.

Thus the strong version suggests that the language we speak determines the nature of our thoughts, including the types of ideas and concepts we are able to have. It proposes that thoughts that are possible in one language may not be possible in another. The weak version, on the other hand, suggests that language has a more subtle effect on thought and merely influences what we are likely to perceive or remember about an object or event. If you have a word for something in your language you are more likely to recognise and remember it than someone who uses a language that does not have a word for it.

More recently Hunt and Agnoli (1991) have suggested an alternative form of the LRH. This is a *cognitive approach* to the relationship between language and thought which focuses on the computational costs that different languages impose on thinking. In other words, the language you speak makes it easier, and therefore more likely, to think in one way or another.

The three versions are discussed below, but before exploring the evidence in detail it should be acknowledged that any version of the hypothesis is difficult to test. One problem, outlined by Boroditsky (2001), is that people are tested in their native language and it may be that the instructions given lead to different ways of approaching the task. We have a common concept of what the word 'same' means in English but does a translation to a different language evoke an identical concept? It may be that the translation to one language means 'identical' but to another 'the most similar'. Secondly, there is a problem of isolating what is the effect of language on thought from the effects of culture and shared experiences amongst people using the same language. Thus, if differences in thought can be identified between two groups, it is difficult to know whether this is the effect of language, culture or both.

The strong hypothesis

The strong version of the LRH, that language determines thought, is usually linked to the work of Whorf (1956). Whorf did a detailed analysis of a number of Native American languages and concluded that the differences in language, both in **grammar** and the number of terms used to refer to objects, must shape the way people think about their world. For example, Whorf noted that Inuits use a number of different words for snow, which indicate whether it is falling snow, slushy snow, and so on, whereas in English there is only one term. Whorf believed that these differences in language would inevitably lead to differences in the way people thought about snow.[1] In another example Whorf reports that Hopi Indians use just one word for anything that flies whether it is a pilot, aeroplane, insect, etc. He also noted differences between Hopi and English grammar. For example, Whorf claimed that the Hopi language was a timeless language since he could find no clear grammatical structure to distinguish past, present and future. In English (and most other languages) the verb structure clearly indicates the tense. Furthermore, in English we tend to talk about time as something that can be quantified objectively (e.g. 'I stayed for 3 hours'). So, for example, days, hours, minutes, etc. are regarded as the same sort of objective data as kilometres, metres and millimetres. In contrast the Hopi tend to refer to time subjectively or how it appears to them (e.g. 'I leave in the evening'). Another grammatical difference is that a number of things that are regarded as objects (nouns) in English are used as verbs in Hopi. English speakers regard lightning, smoke, flames or waves as objects, and we talk of '*some* smoke' or '*a* bolt of lightning'. The Hopi regard such transitory objects/events as verbs and would say 'it smokes' or 'it lights'. Such

---

1 The exact number of terms that Inuits use for snow is disputed and varies with nearly every report. Harley (2001) puts the true figure at two but notes that Whorf claimed there were seven. However, this figure has been inflated from 'more than 20' to 'over 100' in some reports.

differences, Whorf argued, have led to differences in concepts held within each culture and determined the way people think.

Evaluation of the strong hypothesis

There have been very few studies that support the strong version of the LRH, and even these tend to yield ambiguous results. For example, Carroll and Casagrande (1958) compared the development of form and shape recognition between English and Navaho speakers. The Navaho language stresses the importance of form and shape because many verb endings change according to the shape of object. Thus the ending of the verb, to carry, varies when the object being carried is long and rigid (like a stick), long and flexible (like rope) or flat (like a sheet). There is no such emphasis in English. Carroll and Casagrande studied three groups of children; one group that spoke Navaho only (Navaho-Navaho), a second group of Navaho who spoke both Navaho and English (Navaho-English) and a third group of American children of European descent who spoke English only (English). They found that the Navaho-Navaho group developed form recognition earlier than the English group. This seems to be evidence for the strong version of the LRH, since language seems to determine the development of thought in the children. However the Navaho-English group developed form recognition *later* than the English group and this is inconsistent with the theory (they should have been between the Navaho-Navaho group and English group).

The strong version of the LRH has been criticised on a number of grounds. Lenneberg and Roberts (1956) pointed out that Whorf had put forward a circular argument. He argued that because languages differ, thinking must differ. However, he did not *study thought,* and any evidence of differences in thought came from an examination of language. In other words he proposed that there must be differences in thought because he had found differences between languages. Another consistent criticism of Whorf has been of the evidence he used. For example, Garnham and Oakhill (1994) describe how Whorf translated Native American languages into English in a 'simplistic, word-by-word' fashion (p.48). This results in apparently unusual combinations of words which Whorf uses as evidence of differences in thinking. However, anyone who has studied another language soon realises that word-for-word translations do not work since they usually result in nonsense sentences. One of the difficult aspects of learning another language is to understand the *meaning* of idiomatic phrases since literal translations seem meaningless. Imagine, for example, translating the English sentence 'It's raining cats and dogs'. Any literal translation would seem to be very strange. The fact that we can translate the *intended meaning* from one language to another despite the linguistic differences suggests a *universality* of thought. Greene (1975) also criticises the way Whorf translated Native American languages into English. She points out that if we were to do a similar translation from English into Hopi there would be a number of anomalies. For example, English does not use gender terms for objects except for animals and people yet there is a tendency to refer to boats as female ('she's a fast ship'). Should the Hopi conclude that English speakers have a strange belief that boats are female or should they regard it as a figure of speech? Garnham and Oakhill (1994) also believe that Whorf's use of 'evidence' about the different number of words for snow used in Inuit and English is invalid. They argue that differing numbers of words are needed because of the needs of the environment not because of any fundamental differences in thought. They note that one group of English speakers, skiers, do have a number of different words for snow, but these are not equivalent to the Inuit terms because of the differing needs.

There is little or no evidence that language determines thought and any evidence that has been presented is seriously flawed. The strong version of the LRH does not seem to be a plausible theory.

The weak hypothesis

The weak version of the LRH is that language *influences* thought. There are at least two versions of the weak hypothesis: that language influences perception or that language influences memory (Miller and McNeil, 1969, refer to these as the weak and weakest form of the LRH respectively).

Weakest version of LRH

Evidence for the *weakest* form of the LRH, that language influences memory, was revealed in a study by Carmichael *et al.* (1932). They showed participants a series of nonsense pictures (Figure 2.1),

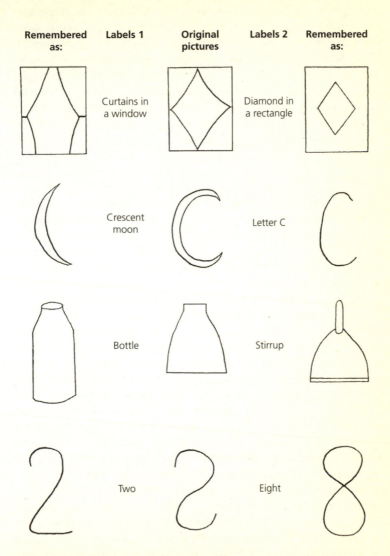

Figure 2.1 **The effect of labels on the subsequent redrawing of pictures. The reproductions of the original pictures in the centre tended to be influenced by the labels they were shown with (based on Carmichael *et al.*, 1932)**

accompanied by a verbal label. However, half the participants saw one set of labels and the other half a different set. The verbal label seemed to influence the memory of the nonsense picture. For example, when shown the first picture in Figure 2.1, accompanied by the label 'curtains in a window', participants were more likely to remember the picture as the drawing on the left. If, however, the label was 'diamond in a rectangle' participants were more likely to remember the picture as the drawing to the right. This seems to show the influence of language on the memory of objects.

Weak version of LRH

The *weak* version of the LRH, that language influences perception, has been studied using cross-cultural studies of colour perception. There are differences in the way that speakers of different languages name colours. Some languages have more labels for basic colours than others do, and there are also differences in the way colours are divided into categories. If language influences perception then presumably the differences in the labels for colour should influence perception of colour. One study compared the recognition of yellows and oranges by speakers of Zuni and English (Lenneberg and Roberts, 1956). The Zuni language only has one term for the yellow–orange region of the spectrum, and Zuni speakers were more likely to make yellow and orange recognition errors. This suggests that language influences perception of colour. Brown and Lenneberg (1954) showed participants a colour chip and then asked them to pick out the same chip from an array of chips. They found that colours are remembered better if there is a simple name for them (e.g. colours like red and blue are remembered better than mixtures of red and blue). This was taken as evidence that language influences colour recognition.

Although the weak version of the LRH was supported by a few studies it was soon challenged by a number of others. Berlin and Kay (1969) compared the basic colour terms used in ninety-eight different languages. They found that there is a systematic way that colour terms are used which followed the hierarchy shown in Figure 2.2. If only two terms are used then these refer to black and white (or light and dark). If a language has three terms they refer to black, white and red. If six terms are used they refer to black, white, red, yellow, blue and green, and so on. In all they found eleven basic terms used to refer to

If eleven	purple	pink	orange	grey
If seven		brown		
If six	yellow	blue		green
If three		red		
If two terms		black	white	

Figure 2.2 **The hierarchy of the eleven basic colour terms (based on Berlin and Kay, 1969)**

colour, and if people from a variety of cultures are asked to pick a colour chip that best represented the colour term they tended to choose similar chips. These colours have been called *focal colours*. Furthermore, people tend to pick out the same eleven colours regardless of how many colour terms there are in their language. This seems to indicate that there are *universal* colour categories that are unaffected by language. In another study Heider (1972) compared English speakers, who use eleven basic colour terms, with Dani speakers who use only two – 'mola' for bright and 'mili' for dark. English speakers remembered the eleven basic (or focal) colours better than non-focal colours (e.g. a pure red is picked out better than a red-orange). Heider found that the same was true of the Dani despite the fact they did not have terms for the focal colours. Again this is strong evidence of colour categories being universal and does not support the LRH.

The studies by Heider (1972) and Berlin and Kay (1969) were very influential, and many did not regard the weak version of the LRH as a credible theory for some time. However, a number of recent studies have questioned the conclusions of the studies and have revived the weak LRH theory. For example, Davies and his colleagues have carried out a number of cross-cultural studies on a variety of colour sorting tasks. Studies by Davies and Corbett (1997) and Davies (1998) compared speakers of Setswana, English and Russian since these languages differ in the number of terms used for colour, particularly in the blue–green region. Setswana has a single term for blue–green colours (botula), English has two (blue and green) and Russian has three (zelenyj: green; sinij: dark blue; goluboj: light blue). The results from these studies revealed two things. Firstly, there was a marked similarity of colour grouping for all languages. This suggests that colour grouping is universal and is inconsistent with the LRH. However, there were also small but reliable differences in grouping in the blue–green region, with Setswana speakers being more likely to group blue and green together. This finding is consistent with the weak version of the LRH. Another study compared Setswana and English speakers on colour triad tasks (Davies *et al.*, 1998). English has eleven basic terms for colour but Setswana has only five. Again the results showed marked similarity in results with small, reliable differences associated with linguistic differences. Davies *et al.* (p.1) concluded:

> there is a strong universal influence on colour choice but this universal influence can be moderated by cultural influences such as language, a position consistent with weak Whorfianism.

Davidoff *et al.*(1999a, 1999b) have studied the Berinmo of Papua New Guinea using similar methods to those used by Heider in his (1972) study of the Dani. However, in contrast to Heider, they did not find evidence that colour categories were universal; rather, they found evidence consistent with the LRH. They identified a colour boundary in English (between blue and green) that does not exist in Berinmo and a similar colour boundary that exists in Berinmo (between 'nol' and 'wor') that does not exist in English. They asked participants to remember a colour over 30 seconds then to select it from two similar alternatives. The English speakers showed an advantage for blue-green decisions and the Berinmo showed an advantage for nol-wor decisions. Davidoff *et al.* (1999a, p.204) claim that their results 'are consistent with there being a considerable degree of linguistic influence on colour categorisation' and therefore support weak LRH.

One of the problems of the weak/weakest version of the LRH is that it is difficult to know exactly what the theory is and therefore what is being tested. The notion that language 'influences thought' is imprecise. It begs the question what is language influencing – all thoughts or certain types of thought? If the latter, then what sort of thoughts are influenced? Hunt and Agnoli (1991) have claimed that the hypothesis that language influences thought is 'so vague that it is unprovable' (p.377). Furthermore, on inspection of some of the studies in this area it becomes difficult to identify whether it is perception or memory of colours that is being investigated. For example, the Davidoff studies looked at the influence of language on the memory of a perceived colour. Is this evidence for the weak or weakest version of the LRH? Thus there is still debate about influence of language on thought, but there does seem to be better evidence for the weakest form of the LRH, that language influences memory.

The cognitive approach

Hunt and Agnoli (1991) believed that, although the traditional view of the weak version of the LRH was unprovable, there was evidence from a variety of sources that showed that language *does* affect thought. They argue that by taking a cognitive approach the effect of a language on thought can be quantified and therefore evaluated (see Key Research Summary, Article 1 'The Whorfian hypothesis: A cognitive psychology perspective', on p.110). Central to their argument is the notion that different languages make certain thoughts easier or harder. Thus some thoughts or lines of reasoning are easier in some languages than others. Hunt and Agnoli refer to the relative ease of thoughts as the *computational cost,* and it is this cost that influences the likelihood of thinking in a particular way. A word or statement may be easy and natural in one language but difficult or unmanageable in a second. A person using the first language is more likely to think about the word or statement because it is less costly. Hunt and Agnoli cite the example of the word *mokita* from the Kiriwina language of New Guinea, which translates into English as 'truth everybody knows but nobody speaks'. In this case the word *mokita* is more economical to use and think about than its English counterpart. Although English speakers can understand the concept it is easier for a Kiriwina speaker to use this concept. Hunt and Agnoli (p.387) conclude:

> Our review has convinced us that different languages pose different challenges for cognition and provide differential support to cognition.

In other words, different languages make it easier or harder to think in certain ways.

Evaluation of the cognitive hypothesis

There are a number of studies that support their hypothesis. Hunt and Agnoli describe differences in arithmetic capability that exist between speakers of different languages. These differences tend to be subtle but nevertheless consistent. For example, English-speaking children have to learn a relatively large number of terms that refer to numbers. In addition to the basic terms of 0–9, 10, 100, etc., English-speaking children have to learn separate words to refer to 11–19 and each decade term (20, 30, etc.). In contrast a child learning Chinese only has to learn fourteen basic terms (0–10, 100, 1,000, 10,000). The number 11 does not have a special term but is referred to as 10 plus 1. When learning arithmetic English-speaking children initially have problems learning the range of numbers in the teens, but Chinese-speaking children do not. This presumably reflects the extra *cost* of learning extra numerical terms. Hunt and Agnoli cite further evidence for the cognitive hypothesis from studies of bilingual participants. For example, Hoffman *et al.* (1986) studied the use of stereotypes in bilingual English–Chinese speakers. They gave the bilingual speakers descriptions of people that conformed to either English or Chinese stereotypes. Later they were asked whether certain behaviours would be characteristic of a person. When asked in English the participants used English stereotypes, but when asked in Chinese they used Chinese stereotypes. Thus the language used seemed to influence the ease of use (*cost*) of a stereotype.

A number of studies have added support to the cognitive version of the LRH by demonstrating the influence of language on different aspects of thought, including spatial thinking, development of concepts and conceptions of time. For example, Boroditsky (2001) compared conceptions of time between Mandarin and English speakers. She found that English and Mandarin speakers refer to time in a different way and, in a series of studies, found that this difference was reflected in the way that people thought about time. She drew two main conclusions from the studies:

1. Language 'is a powerful tool in shaping thought' about abstract ideas (p.1).
2. Native language is important in 'shaping habitual thought' (p.1).

These conclusions are consistent with the cognitive view of the LRH.

Although the cognitive approach of Hunt and Agnoli (1991) has reawakened interest in the LRH it has not received unconditional support, and there are some elements of the theory that have not been fully investigated. For example, Eysenck and Keane (2000) point out that although Hunt and Agnoli emphasise the importance of 'computational costs' this has not been quantified in the studies. Until these costs can be quantified there is essentially little difference between the weak and cognitive versions of the LRH. Also, as with all forms of the LRH, when comparing speakers from different cultures it is difficult to isolate any effect of language from other cultural influences.

LRH: summary

1. There seems to be little evidence for the *strong version* of the LRH and there is a consensus of opinion that language does not *determine* thought.
2. There is a variety of evidence for the *weak version* of the LRH, but this version – that language influences thought – is vague. There seems to be better evidence that language influences some aspects of thought (e.g. memory) more than other aspects (e.g. perception).
3. The *cognitive version* of the LRH – that a speaker's language makes some thoughts more difficult (or costly) than they would be in another language – is currently generating a lot of interest. Some research seems to support this version.

Review the LRH by answering the following questions:

1. What are two of the main problems of the strong version of the LRH?
2. What is the difference between the weak and the weakest version of the LRH?
3. Describe one cross-cultural study that supports the cognitive version of the LRH.

Progress exercise

Thought determines language

The theory that language depends on thought is associated with Piaget (1950, 1967). Piaget studied cognitive development in children and believed that development takes place in a number of stages (this is described in detail in the forthcoming book *Cognitive Development* in this series). These stages are sequential and at each stage a child acquires new cognitive skills. For example at about 10 months of age children develop **object permanence**, a recognition that objects still exist even if they cannot be seen. Piaget believed that language development was as a result of cognitive development. In other words, *language is dependent on the type of thoughts* a child has. In order to use language appropriately a child must first develop the ideas or concepts. Piaget noted that a child might use words before understanding what they mean but that this is not using true language. A child may merely repeat words, or play with words, without understanding the concept that this is merely **egocentric speech** which is not intended to convey information. In adult language the purpose of speech is to convey ideas or information and it is social. Speech can only be used in this way if the child understands what the word/s refer to. For example, a child may use the word 'bigger' after hearing an adult say it but cannot use the word to communicate about the *concept* of bigger until this concept has developed. Thus suggests that the thought or concept determines the use of language.

Studies of development

A variety of studies support this theory. One group of studies has compared the development of concepts in children with their use of language. For example, Tomasello and Farrar (1986) studied the comprehension of relational words ('gone', 'down', 'up') during the development of object permanence. They found that words that indicate change to the object while it is still present ('up', 'down') were understood before words which relate to absent objects ('gone'). Sinclair-de-Zwart (1969) studied a group of children and firstly determined whether they could 'conserve'. This is the ability to realise that when something changes shape it does not change in mass or volume (e.g. a thin tube of water poured into a squat beaker changes shape but does not change in volume). She found that children who could conserve understood words and phrases such as 'bigger' or 'as much as' but that the children who could not conserve did not understand the words. Furthermore, even if the children who could not conserve were given language training relating to these words they still did not use them correctly. These studies suggest the concept must emerge before a child can use the language relating to the concept.

Another way of investigating Piaget's theory is to compare the cognitive development and language development of children when one of these abilities is impaired (Harley, 2001). If language development does depend on cognitive development then impairment of language development should have little or no impact on cognitive development. However, if cognitive development is impaired it should have an effect on language development. A variety of studies show that, in general, this is the case. For example, language development can be impaired in deaf children but a number of studies have shown that their cognitive development is normal (e.g. Furth, 1971). In contrast, impairment of cognitive development is often linked to impairment of language. Harley (2001) points out that there is some correlation between cognitive skills and language skills. Generally, children with learning difficulties develop language slower than other children do. However, one must be cautious in drawing conclusions from these studies since they are correlational. Correlations do not show cause and effect (i.e. that impairment of thought development causes impairment of language difficulties) and it is possible that both the learning and language impairments are caused by another factor.

Problems of Piaget's theory

Although Harley (2001) has showed that there is a general link between cognitive and language developments there are a number of exceptions. For example, Yamanda (1990) has reported a case study of 'Laura' who had severe learning difficulties but normal language development. Laura had an IQ estimated at 41; she showed problems with most cognitive tasks yet was able to perform complex linguistic tasks. Yamanda believes that this suggests that cognitive processes (thought) and language are distinct. Bellugi *et al.* (1991) have studied children with Williams syndrome. This syndrome causes impairment to cognitive abilities and low IQ levels but does not affect language skills (in fact people with Williams syndrome seem to enjoy using language and use it well). Both these studies suggest language is not dependent on thought but rather that the two abilities are *separate*.

Another problem of Piaget's theory is that it seems to under-estimate the role of language in promoting cognitive and social development. Some studies suggest that, rather than just being a product of cognitive development, acquisition of language skills can accelerate cognitive development. For example, Luria and Yudovich (1971) have reported the cases of twin boys who at the age of 5 had very poor language and cognitive skills because of an unstimulating environment. They were placed in separate homes and one twin was given special training in language but the other was not. The twin given language training made more rapid progress in a variety of other ways. This study suggests that, rather than being simply a result of cognitive development, acquiring language *promotes* cognitive development.

Progress exercise

Briefly explain why:

1. The study by Sinclair-de-Zwart (1969) supports Piaget's theory.
2. The study by Yamanda (1990) does not support Piaget's theory.

The interdependence of language and thought

Vygotsky (1962) studied child development and, based on his observations of children's early speech and monologues, proposed a complex theory of the interaction between thought and language (this is also described in the forthcoming *Cognitive Development* book in this series). He suggested that initially thought and language are *independent* and have separate origins. During this stage thoughts are non-verbal and are primarily based on images whilst language is pre-intellectual and is not linked to thought. At around the age of 2 thought and language start to become connected, and children start to use language in their thoughts and their speech begins to represent their thoughts. Language and thought start to become *interdependent*. However, the interdependence of language and thought is not an instantaneous process and the two gradually become more and more interdependent between the ages of 2 and 7. Vygotsky believes that language has two functions, to communicate to others (an external function) and to monitor thoughts (an internal function). Adults are generally good at separating the two functions but children up to the age of 7 can find this difficult. Between the ages of 2 and 7 children often talk about their ideas and thoughts and as a result communication can be confused. Like Piaget, Vygotsky called this type of speech egocentric but in contrast to Piaget he saw egocentric speech as a form of self-guidance which occurs because it has not been internalised. Vygotsky stressed the importance of language in the cognitive development of children and the interdependence of language and thought. He claimed that:

> The relation of thought and word is not a thing but a process, a continual movement back and forth from thought to language and from word to thought.
>
> (Vygotsky, 1972, p.186)

Vygotsky developed his ideas from his observations of children and their use of language. If a young child is given a difficult task to perform they will often talk through the solution. This use of speech is not used to communicate but to direct and monitor thoughts and seems to show the confusion between the internal and external functions of language. He believed inner speech can be studied through egocentric speech and is therefore available to observation and experimentation. The theory is also supported by evidence that language skills can help enhance cognitive development (e.g. Luria and Yudovich, 1971).

One problem in evaluating Vygotsky's theory is that, although he described his ideas in detail, he did not describe the detail of the methods he used in his studies of children. It is therefore difficult to replicate his findings and, in Harley's (2001) view, difficult to assess.

Summary

There are a number of views on the nature of the relationship between language and thought. One view, the linguistic relativity hypothesis (LRH), is that the language a speaker uses affects the way the speaker thinks. There seems to be little evidence for the strongest form of the LRH; that is, that language *determines* thought. The original evidence used by Whorf was flawed and no evidence has emerged subsequently that fully supports the strong version. The evidence about the weak version of the LRH, that language *influences* thought, is much less clear-cut. There seems to be some evidence that language influences memory and perception, but the vagueness of the hypothesis makes the extent of the influence of language difficult to quantify. The recent introduction of a cognitive perspective has revived this debate and there is growing evidence that the language a person uses does affect the way information is processed. However, the cognitive approach has not received unconditional support. Studies of child development led Piaget to believe that language is dependent upon thoughts. His theory suggests that language cannot be used to communicate ideas until the child has developed the appropriate concepts. There is some evidence that children need to understand concepts before using language about these concepts. However, some children with learning difficulties are capable of a sophisticated level of language despite impairments to most other cognitive functions. Vygotsky believes that language and thought are initially independent and separate but that during childhood thought gradually becomes more and more verbal and that language requires and reflects thoughts. By the age of 7 thought and language become interlinked and interdependent. Vygotsky's ideas have generated much interest and seem to explain some aspects of children's behaviour, but the studies he used to support his ideas have been difficult to replicate.

Fill in the blank areas in the table below.

	Description of theory	Supported by	Criticised by
Strong LRH			Greene (1975) Garnham and Oakhill (1994)
Weak LRH	Language influences thoughts		
Cognitive LRH		Hoffman, et al. (1986)	
Piaget			
Vygotsky			
		Luria and Yudovich (1971)	

Further reading

Garnham, A. and Oakhill, J. (1994) *Thinking and Reasoning*. Oxford: Blackwell. Although this book is primarily about thinking and problem-solving it does have a good chapter on the relationship between language and thought.

Harley, T.A. (2001) *The Psychology of Language: From data to theory* (2nd edn). Hove: Psychology Press. This book has a very good chapter on the relationship between language and thought. Although the book is aimed at undergraduates it is clear and logical.

3

Social and cultural aspects of language

Introduction
Social class
Ethnic background
Gender
Summary
Review exercise

Introduction

One of the topics in the previous chapter was the influence on thought of using different languages. However, there are also great differences in the use of any one language within a culture, and the way we speak reflects our cultural and social background. There are variations of language that are caused by a range of factors such as class, ethnic origin, gender, age and geographical region. In addition the language we use is not fixed and we tend to use different styles of language to suit the situation. For example, students will use different language when they are out with their friends than when discussing an essay with their lecturer, switching from an informal to a more formal style.

The social and cultural variations in language give rise to a number of questions. Firstly, what is the nature of the differences between different social and cultural groups? Secondly, do the variations in language affect cognition? This question links to the discussion of the weak version of the linguistic relativity hypothesis in the previous chapter but instead of looking at the differences between languages looks at the differences between versions of the same language. A final question is what is the social impact of the differences in language? For example, do variations in language influence the perception of individuals or groups? This chapter will focus on three social and cultural aspects of language: social class, ethnic background and gender.

Social class

In the 1960s Bernstein, a British sociologist, began to look at the link between language, class and education. He suggested that generally working-class and middle-class children use two different types of language: **restricted code** and **elaborated code** respectively (Bernstein, 1961, 1971). Restricted code consists of short sentences with a relatively simple form of grammar. There tends to be a greater use of pronouns than nouns, and the restricted code therefore tends to be context bound (because references to 'it' or 'them', etc. can only be understood in context). Elaborated code, on the other hand, consists of longer sentences with complex grammar. There are more adjectives and a greater use of nouns as opposed to pronouns, which makes it context independent. Bernstein (2000, p.451) illustrated the two codes with two stories which were written about the same set of four pictures.

a) They're playing football and he kicks it and it goes through there it breaks the window and they're looking at it and he comes out and shouts at them because they've broken it so they runaway and then she looks out and she tells them off.

b) Three boys are playing football and one boy kicks the ball and it goes through the window the ball breaks the window and the boys are looking at it and a man comes out and shouts at them because they've broken the window so they run away and then that lady looks out of her window and she tells the boys off.

Story (a) illustrates the restricted code as it uses a lot of pronouns and is difficult to understand without the pictures (context bound). Story (b) illustrates the elaborated code; it uses more nouns and can be followed without seeing the pictures (context independent). Bernstein (1971) claimed that working-class children have limited access to elaborated code and because of socialisation are largely limited to using the restricted code.

Bernstein believed that the different codes have both cognitive and educational consequences. One consequence was that children do not develop their full cognitive potential using restricted code. In this respect Bernstein's view is like the LRH in that it suggests that different forms of language lead to different ways of thinking. He used evidence from intelligence tests and found that there was little difference between the verbal and non-verbal scores for middle-class children, but in working-class children the verbal scores were often much lower than the non-verbal scores. Bernstein believed this was a consequence of using the restricted code. The different codes also have implications for education and may help to explain why working-class children generally do not do as well as the middle-class children at school. Teachers use a formal, elaborated code to communicate to their pupils, and children who are used to a restricted code find this difficult to understand. Restricted code users are in effect being taught in another language.

Bernstein's ideas have been strongly criticised for a number of reasons. One of his strongest critics, Labov suggested that Bernstein shows a bias against working-class behaviour and that he portrays middle-class language as being superior. Labov (1972), on the other hand, believed that the language of working class was not 'restricted' but different (see p.32 for a description of Labov's view of language). He argued that rather than regarding middle-class language as superior it could be seen as 'turgid, redundant, bombastic and empty' (2000, p.459). Just because something is elaborate does not make it superior. Labov also criticised the methodology Bernstein used to collect data because he used formal interviews to collect information about language. However, this is precisely the sort of situation where one might expect the working-class children to feel inhibited in using language. In addition the interviewers were middle-class and the middle-class children could relate to them much more easily. Even if a link could be established between use of restricted code and poor school performance Bernstein did not show what the nature of this link is (i.e. he did not show cause and effect). Furthermore, the differences in the verbal and non-verbal intelligence scores found in the working-class children using the restricted code might reflect a cultural bias in the verbal test. Tests tend to be constructed by middle-class psychologists and therefore are designed using elaborated code and will yield higher scores from children using elaborated code. Finally there is a problem in allocating children's language into one of two codes since there is such variety in the way they use language.

Ethnic background

Labov (1972), like Bernstein, was interested in the language differences between groups in society. He studied the language used by African-American children in New York and found that, contrary to popular belief, the language used was not a substandard form of English but an alternative form. He suggests that the negative view of their language came from educational psychologists who knew very little about African-American children and that to understand the verbal capabilities of children they need to be studied in their own cultural context. The children used a different dialect of English he called Black English Vernacular (BEV). Labov showed that BEV is as creative and rich as Standard English and uses some different, but consistent, grammatical rules. For example, Labov found there are some differences in the use of verbs and a tendency to use double negatives in sentences. He points out that, although the use of something like a double negative is not used in Standard English, it is a logical way of expressing an idea. Wolfram (1997) also showed that BEV uses consistent grammatical rules. For example, the tendency to use the word 'be' instead of 'is' is linked to actions that occur a number of times not to actions that happen only once. Thus a group of African-American children judged the sentence 'When we play basketball, she be on my team' to be correct but not the sentence 'The girl in the picture be my sister'.

Work has continued on BEV in America and there is a large body of work both on the language and on its influence in education (see, for example, Wolfram *et al.*, 1999). BEV has been referred to as Ebonics (literally Black Sounds) but the preferred term in America now is African-American Vernacular English (AAVE). Research has shown that dialect differences can affect both the academic and social quality of some children's education (Labov, 1995). Children who use 'non-standard' dialects typically have poorer educational attainment.

There have been court cases in the USA where African-American parents have sued local school groups because they believed their children were being denied equal educational opportunities since the school did not take into account the children's vernacular. The use of AAVE in teaching has sparked an intense debate in the USA following Oakland Unified School District's decision in 1996 to use AAVE in teaching the African-American children. In the district over half the student population is African-American, but generally they are doing poorly in schools. The Oakland decision was to use AAVE as a means of educating the children and to improve their Standard English. This provoked a debate in which some claimed that it was political correctness going to far. However, Christian (1997) suggests that the negative attitudes about AAVE stem from a mistaken belief that it is inferior rather than different. Adger (1997) points out that the idea that there is a Standard English in the USA is a myth and suggests that an active study of dialects benefits *all* students not just African-American students.

In conclusion, although there is little evidence that using different dialects affects cognition there is a wealth of evidence showing it does have important implications in education. Students using a non-standard dialect, like AAVE, tend not to reach their potential if the educational system is geared towards a different dialect.

Labov argues that BEV (or AAVE) is an alternative form of Standard English that is vibrant and creative. Think of some of the words and phrases from AAVE that are now part of Standard English. (You may find listening to some African-American music artists useful for this exercise!)

Progress exercise

Gender

In recent years there has been growing interest in gender differences in language. These differences affect both the content and the style of language used and have been called **genderlect** (Owens, 2001). These differences start early and by the age of 4 to 5 children's language starts to reflect the gender differences found in adults (Haas, 1975). This is not surprising as the style of parental speech to infants varies according to gender from a very early age (Owens, 2001). For example, fathers tend to use more commands to boys and use more insulting terms to them than they do to girls (Berko Gleason and Greif, 1983). This is reflected in the differences in male to male and male to female adult conversations. However, before looking at these differences in detail it is worth pointing out that there are more similarities than differences in language and that any analysis of gender and language styles has to take account of cultural background (Tannen, 1994). It should also be obvious that any gender differences are generalised and are not apparent in all women or all men.

Deficit model

One of the first people systematically to study the differences between female and male language was Lakoff (1975). Lakoff claims that these differences show up in all levels of language from the type of words to the type of syntax. She suggests that men are more likely to use stronger expletives than women. For example, if presented with two sentences: (a) 'Oh dear, you've put the peanut butter in the refrigerator again' or (b) 'Shit, you've put the peanut butter in the refrigerator again', we are likely to judge that the first was spoken by a woman and the second by a man. Lakoff describes differences in the tag questions used by men and women and that women use them in a way that lacks authority (e.g. 'that'll be alright, won't it?'). She believes that women are socialised into using language that reflects the social inequalities between the sexes. However, Cameron (1995) has claimed that in characterising women's language as lacking authority Lakoff has presented a negative assessment of women's language. She has also criticised Lakoff for dealing in stereotypes (Cameron, 1985). Cameron (1995) describes Lakoff's position as being a *deficit* model of gender and language. In other words it describes women's language as being disadvantaged because it lacks some of the features of the language used by men (i.e. similar to Bernstein's view of working-class language). There is also concern that the examples used by Lakoff to support her arguments have dated (e.g. Burke *et al.*, 2000). For example, one of the ideas discussed is that there are some prohibitions about women's language (such as swearing) that do not apply to men's language. However, many of these do not seem to apply today and may reflect a change in culture.

Cultural differences model

An alternative approach has been put forward by Tannen (1990, 1994) who has outlined two different conversational styles between women and men but regards both as being equally valid. Cameron (1995) describes this position as a *cultural difference* model since it regards gender differences in language as being analogous to differences to other cultural influences such as ethnicity (e.g. Labov; see p.32). Tannen (1994) suggests that women tend to be more indirect than men and seek to find connections and consensus. Men, on the other hand, tend to use conversations as a means of conveying information and use language to maintain status and independence. Owens (2001) notes that amongst men the topics of conversation are rarely about feelings and as a consequence men rarely experience intimacy in adulthood. In contrast a common feature of women's conversation is the sharing of emotions (Tannen, 1994). This seems to suggest a different role in conversations, women tend to be more supportive and men more combative. Tannen (1990) claims that although both styles of language are equally valid the differences are a frequent source of misunderstandings between women and men.

Cameron (1995) has criticised this view on several levels. Firstly she points out that the suggestion that men have one style and women another is overgeneralised and stereotypical since both women and men use a wide variety of styles in conversation. She also notes that where differences do occur they stem from unequal gender relations and that simply accepting that there are differences in language does not address these inequalities. Cameron (1995, p.42) claims 'Tannen's relativism perpetuates women's exclusion from languages of power, while failing to challenge any of the masculine behaviours which reinforce that exclusion.'

Sexism in language

A different issue in the study of gender and language is the issue of sexism in language. It is argued that the way language is used (by both men and women) can promote stereotyped views of gender and present males as the most important sex. Spender (1990), in her book *Man Made Language,* looks at the sexism of language and argues that language is man-made and promotes male dominance. She suggests that 'males, as the dominant group, have produced language, thought and reality' (p.143). For example, students learning subjects such as science or social science, where the term 'man' was used to represent humans (i.e. the evolution of man, urban man, etc.), tended to have an image of a male not male and female. Thus the language used promotes a perception that males are the most important sex.

Spender's arguments are very similar to the weak version of the LRH since she argues that language influences our perception and memory of the world.

Summary

Language is affected by social and cultural factors such as social class, ethnic background and gender. Bernstein suggested that working-class and middle-class children use different language codes which he called restricted and elaborate. Restricted code uses short sentences, a lot of pronouns and is context-bound, whereas elaborated code uses longer sentences with more complex grammar and is context-independent. Bernstein believes that the use of restricted code is the cause of educational underachievement in working-class children. Labov strongly disagrees with some of Bernstein's conclusions. After studying the language of African-American children he believes it is a mistake to view working-class language as restricted or inferior. Rather, there are different dialects that use some different rules but are just as rich as Standard English. He called the African-American dialect Black English Vernacular (BEV) but the preferred term is now African-American Vernacular English (AAVE). AAVE continues to be an important field of study with wide-reaching educational implications. Gender differences in the use of language start in childhood and these differences affect both the content (vocabulary) and the conversational style of speech. Lakoff believes women are socialised into using a style of speech that lacks authority and this reflects the inequalities between the sexes in society. This has been criticised as stereotypical and a negative view of women's language. Tannen suggests that women and men use two different styles of language, both equally valid. This has also been criticised as being stereotypical and overgeneralised. Furthermore, this view can be seen as a justification for accepting inequalities.

Review exercise

Review the sections on social class and ethnicity and identify the educational implications of Bernstein's view and Labov's view of language and culture.

What are the social implications of Lakoff's and Tannen's views of gender and language?

Further reading

Burke, L., Crowley, T. and Girvin, A. (2000) *The Routledge Language and Cultural Theory Reader.* London: Routledge. This is a useful book for students who wish to read some of the original work in this area. It has articles by Bernstein, Labov, Lakoff and Spender on the social and cultural aspects of language.

4

Language acquisition

Introduction
The stages of language acquisition
Pre-linguistic stage
One-word stage
Development of grammar
Meaning and pragmatics
Summary
Review exercise

Introduction

The use of language is an extraordinarily complicated skill. Each of us has the capacity to produce and understand an almost limitless number of sentences. For many people this skill for using language is a defining feature of humanity. Yet this complicated skill seems to be learned by children with no difficulty, and nearly all children who are exposed to language learn it very quickly.

There are a large number of studies of language development in children. Some of this research is cross-sectional (studying groups of children of different ages), but due to the complexity of language learning and the variation between children a lot of the work is longitudinal. These are studies of children over a long period of time and typically concentrate on one or two children. The research into the process of language learning has led to a number of theories about how children learn language. This chapter will focus on the *process* of language learning and the next will consider *theories* of how children learn language.

The stages of language acquisition

There is great variation in language acquisition in children. They vary in the speed they learn, the words they learn, etc. These variations can be biological, social or cultural in origin. However, despite these variations it seems that all children learn language in a number of stages. These stages appear to be universal and apply to all children regardless of the language they are learning or the society they are in. The three main stages that have been identified are the **pre-linguistic stage**, **one-word stage** and development of grammar (starting with two-word stage). There are two things to bear in mind when looking at stages of language development. Firstly, the transition from one stage to the next is very gradual. A child who starts to use two-word sentences will carry on using one-word utterances for some time. Secondly, because of the variation at which children learn language, the ages given for each stage are a very rough guide only.

Pre-linguistic stage

The pre-linguistic stage is the time before children start to use their first words and lasts from birth to approximately 12 months old. Although children of this age do not use language this is an important stage for both comprehension and production of language. A large number of studies have shown that infants are very sensitive to the sounds made in speech and are able to distinguish between similar consonant or syllable sounds from as little as 1 month old. For example, Eimas *et al*. (1971) found that 1-month-old infants were able to differentiate between a 'pa' and 'ba' sound. Initially infants do not use a wide range of sounds and until about 2 months old the principal sound they produce is *crying*. Infants do communicate using crying and parents become skilled at determining different types of cry. At about 2 months old infants add a different type of sound to their repertoire which is called *cooing*. These are vowel sounds such as 'oooo' which vary in tone and volume. Cooing is typically associated with pleasure.

A major development in the production of speech sounds occurs at about 6 months when infants start to produce sounds which combine vowels and consonants (e.g. 'ga' or 'ba'). The production of these sounds is called **babbling** and this accounts for a large part of the infant's vocalisation from 6 months through to the production of words. The onset of babbling and the types of sounds produced seem to be universal and are similar regardless of culture or of whether the child can hear or not. This suggests that babbling is the result of maturational processes rather than learning. However, there is evidence that infants learn from the sounds they hear because after about 10 months the range of sounds produced is influenced by the sounds of the language the infant hears (de Boysson-Bardies *et al.*, 1984). Infants stop using some of the sounds that they do not hear but carry on using sounds they do hear. Deaf infants tend to stop babbling, presumably because of a lack of feedback. Another feature of babbling at about 10 months is that infants often string lots of babbling sounds together (e.g. 'dadadada'), a characteristic known as **echolalia**. Sequences of echolalia sometimes show intonational patterns which appear speech-like although the infant does not use any words. These patterns reflect the intonational patterns of the language the infants are exposed to (Bee, 2000).

There is a question about how much infants learn about speech production during this phase, but at the very least they seem to learn how to control their vocal tracts and how to produce relevant sounds (Clark and Clark, 1977). There is also evidence that infants understand many words before they are able to produce them (Bee, 2000). This is a feature of all the early stages of language development; the ability to understand speech (receptive language) exceeds the ability to produce speech (expressive language). Another feature of the pre-linguistic stage is that at about 9 months old infants start to communicate using gestures. An infant who points to a toy and makes grasping movements of the hand is clearly 'asking' for the toy (the persistence of the gesture and the loud noise that ensues if the 'request' is not met leave little room for doubt!).

One-word stage

The one-word stage typically starts at about 12 months old. At this age the majority of vocalisation is still babbling, but children start to use words amongst the babbling. Often these early words are not like the adult versions of the word but are approximations of them. Some early words may be totally different to adult versions, but they are regarded as 'words' provided they are used consistently to refer to a specific object or action. For example, Scollon (1976) studied a child named Brenda, one of whose first words was 'nene' which, although bearing little relationship to adult English, was used consistently to refer to anything that was in a feeding bottle (milk, juice, etc.).

After producing the first word the rate of acquisition of new words is initially very slow. For example, one study found that it took 3–4 months after the first word before a further ten words were added (Nelson, 1973). However, at some point between 16 and 18 months children start to acquire new words much more rapidly. Harley (2001) has called this the 'vocabulary explosion' and notes that it coincides with a number of other major language developments such as the production of two-word sentences (see p.43, this volume). The estimates of how many words children produce from 12 months onwards vary greatly and probably reflect the variation amongst children, but typically at 18 months children have a vocabulary of 50 words and at 24 months 300 words. Although there is variation in the actual words that children learn there seems to be a consistent pattern in the types of words they learn. Nelson (1973) found that children's vocabularies in the one-word stage could be classified into six categories, including general nominals (names of objects, e.g. bottle), specific nominals (names unique to people or animals, e.g. Fido), and action words (describing action, e.g. look). She found that over half the words children use are general nominals; subsequent studies suggest this is a trend in many languages, including Japanese, Chinese, German and Turkish. Many early words are often *context-bound* and may be used in certain situations only. For example, Bloom (1973) described a child who only used the word 'car' to describe cars seen from one location.

Although children initially communicate using single words they are able to convey a variety of messages with each word. The message the word conveys may change according to the context in which it is used, the tone in which it is said and the gestures that accompany it. For example a child may use the sound 'di' to refer to a doll. If the word is used with a rising voice whilst pointing to the doll across the room it suggests a request for the doll. The use of single words to convey a variety of messages is known as using **holophrases**.

Think of how a child might indicate the following phrases using just one word:

- This is my juice.
- I want some juice.
- I've spilt my juice.

What other cues would the child use apart from the word itself?

Development of grammar

At about 18 months old children start to produce two-word sentences. This **two-word stage** marks the development of **syntax** (or the grammatical rules of how to combine words). Once they start to combine words children learn grammar very quickly and pass through a number of phases that are characterised by increasing complexity of the grammar and sentence length. Although initially children may use single-word holophrases and some two-word sentences they soon start to use three, then four words, and so on. Psycholinguists use a measure called the mean length of utterance (MLU) to record the average number of words children use in their sentences.

Of course, children continue to add to their vocabulary during this stage and studies show that the rate of word acquisition in pre-school children is remarkable. At the age of 2 children have a vocabulary of about 300 words, but by the age of 6 this increases to an average of 13,000 words.

Early grammar

The use of early grammar, which Brown (1973) called 'Stage 1 grammar', typically lasts from 18 to 30 months (although the transition to later stages is difficult to pinpoint). Sentences during this phase show two main characteristics: they are short and they are simple. Most sentences during this phase are two or three words long and consist of only the essential words to convey meaning (nouns, verbs and adjectives). Many features of adult language are not used. For example, a child may say 'Play doll' instead of 'I am playing with the dolls'. This type of speech has been described as **telegraphic** because, like a telegraph, it uses only the critical words in the sentence (Brown, 1973). Inflections, such as the auxiliary verb 'am' or the plural 's', are omitted.

Although these early sentences are short and simple they seem to be created using rules (or grammar). Owens (2001) suggests that children may experiment with a variety of rules as they start to combine words but eventually use word-order rules such as action + object (e.g. 'drink milk'). These grammatical rules may not be the same as those used by adults but most research suggests that they are used consistently. Thus, although there is not complete agreement about the nature of the early grammar, there seems to be agreement that children use some form of rules for word position. Bee (2000, p.236) claims 'there is no dispute about the assertion that even at this earliest stage children create sentences following rules'.

Later grammar

At about 30 months children start to use more complex grammar and begin what has been called a 'grammar explosion' (Bee, 2000). The length of the sentences (the MLU) gradually gets longer and children start to add both inflections and functional words. Brown (1973) calls the use of more elaborate grammar 'Stage 2 grammar'. In English one of the first inflections to be added is the verb ending 'ing' (e.g. play*ing*), followed by articles (*a* and *the*) and later adding 's' to indicate a plural (e.g. dog*s*). Children also start to use different forms of sentences such as negatives and questions, although the initial form may not be exactly the same as adult language. For example when children first produce negative sentences they often omit the auxiliary verb so they might say 'I not playing' instead of 'I *am* not playing' (Bloom, 1991).

There is evidence that children learn rules of grammar rather than simply imitate adult speech. One source of evidence comes from studies of **overregularisation**. This occurs when regular rules of grammar are applied to irregular examples. For example, adding 'ed' to the end creates the past tense of many verbs (e.g. laughed, played)

– but this is not the case for all verbs. However, children often overregularise and say 'goed' instead of 'went' or 'singed' instead of 'sang'. This is also evident in the use of plurals, which are typically produced by adding an 's'. Children misapply this rule and will say words like 'sheeps' or 'foots'. Another common type of overregularisation occurs in the use of superlatives (as in big, bigger and biggest). Children often misapply the regular rule to the word 'bad' and say 'badder' and 'baddest' instead of worse and worst. Since children will not hear adults using words like 'goed' or 'badder' it seems that they have learned a rule and are misapplying it.

There is also experimental evidence that children learn general language rules. In a famous study Berko (1958) showed children a picture of a fictitious creature called a 'wug' (see Figure 4.1). The children were told 'This is a wug' and then were shown a picture of two of the creatures. After explaining that there was now another wug, the children were asked to complete the sentence 'There are two . . . ' The children responded by saying 'wug**s**'. This clearly shows the

Here is a wug.

Now there is another one.
There are two _____

Figure 4.1 An experiment to test whether children use rules of grammar (based on Berko, 1958; courtesy of Jean Berko Gleason)

application of a rule since the children had never come across a wug before and could not have heard anyone else say 'wugs'.

Language gradually becomes more and more complex in pre-school children. The length of sentences tends to increase and children become able to add ideas together by using conjunctions such as *and*. By the age of about 5 years children tend to learn most of the grammar they will use as adults. However, there are some forms of sentences that are not learned until later. For example 5-year-old children do not use many passive sentences such as 'The cat was chased by the dog.' Furthermore, they can be confused about the meaning of passive sentences, and in the example given they are likely to think that it was the cat that did the chasing. However, adults rarely use passive forms of sentences and it is unlikely that children hear many passive sentences.

Meaning and pragmatics

The discussion in this chapter so far has concentrated on the use of words and production of sentences. There are two other important aspects of learning a language however: developing an understanding of *word meaning* and using language to communicate with others (*pragmatics*).

Meaning

One of the fundamental questions about language is how do children develop an understanding of word meaning? In other words, how do children learn that one particular set of sounds refers to a category of objects or type of action? Initially this seems a simple task to explain; parents use words when objects appear or actions occur. However, take the example of a cat chasing a ball across a room and a parent pointing and saying 'cat'. How does the child know the word refers to the cat? It could refer to something else in the scene (e.g. the ball); it could refer to part of the cat (e.g. the tail); it could refer to a property of the cat (e.g. furriness); or it could refer to something the cat is doing (e.g. running). It is not known exactly how children learn the meaning of words but their behaviour suggests that a number of assumptions or principles are used. Owens (2001) suggests that three of these principles are fundamental to learning word meaning. The first of these, the reference principle, is that words refer to things (i.e. the word 'cat' refers to an animal). Initially this principle is accompanied by the mutual exclusivity assumption or the assumption that a word refers to one class of object only (i.e. the word 'cat' can only refer to the animal and not something else as well such as the ball). The second principle is the extendability principle, which is the assumption that words refer to a class of objects not a unique object (i.e. the word 'cat' refers to all cats not just one cat). The third principle is the whole-object principle, which is that words refer to the whole object not just parts of it (i.e. the word 'cat' refers to the whole animal not the tail). Learning the words that refer to the constituent parts is a later development. Finally, Owens (2001) also notes that children do not simply learn the meaning of words by exposure to them but are actively engaged in trying to understand adult language and to make associations between words and objects.

Another question about learning word meaning is whether children develop a concept about a category first and then the word to describe that category, or whether they learn a word and then the category to which it applies. In other words, does a child discover that there is a group of objects that are furry, have four legs and which bark and then find that there is a word, 'dog', to describe this group or does the child learn the word 'dog' and then find it applies to furry, four-legged objects that bark? (See Chapter 2 about the relationship between language and thought.) There seems to be evidence that both occur, sometimes children learn the concept then the word, but sometimes they learn the word then the concept (Bee, 2000). For example, there is evidence that children cannot use some words accurately until they have developed the appropriate concept (see p.22). On the other hand there is also evidence that when children learn a new word it suggests to them that another category exists (Waxman and Hall, 1993).

Pragmatics

Another vital aspect of language learning is the use of language to communicate with others – pragmatics. There is growing interest in this aspect of language and it lies at the heart of some theories of language learning (see p.61). Children learn some communication skills at an early age but others take more time to develop. For example, children learn the communication skill of turn-taking by 18 months. They are able to use the non-verbal signals of shifting eye gaze to indicate the beginning and end of utterances (Bee, 2000). The use of different types of speech for different audiences comes later, but by the age of 4 children use different speech for adults than they use with younger children. They use a simpler form of language, or 'motherese' (see p.54) with younger children. Most of the skills used in communicating with others are learned by the age of 5.

Summary

Language development occurs in a series of stages. The first stage is the pre-linguistic stage and it lasts from birth to approximately 12 months old. Initially the only sounds infants make is when crying, but within a few weeks they begin cooing. At about 6 months old infants begin babbling. These are vowel and consonant sounds that account for a large part of the infant's vocalisation until the infant begins to use words. The production of words, typically at 12 months old, marks the transition to the next stage, the one-word stage. Acquisition of new words is slow at first and most of these tend to be general nominals (nouns). Children are able to convey a variety of meanings using single words by changing tone or using gestures. The use of single words in this way is called holophrases. Acquisition of new words is initially slow but shortly before 18 months old there is a rapid acceleration that is followed by the emergence of two-word sentences. The use of two-word sentences marks the start of grammar development since the child uses rules to combine the words. Early sentences are described as telegraphic speech because they use only the essential words to communicate meaning. At approximately 30 months old children start to use more complicated grammar and longer sentences. Most of the grammatical rules used as adults are learned by the age of 5, although the use of language continues to become more complex during childhood. Two other important aspects of language are the acquisition of word meaning and pragmatics. Learning of word meaning seems to follow a number of basic principles and involves an active attempt by children to connect words with referents. The skills needed to communicate with others, or pragmatics, are apparent in early childhood and, like grammatical rules, most are learned by the age of 5.

Each box beside the timeline below represents the approximate age for the emergence of an aspect of vocalisation or language. Use the chapter to fill in each box

```
0
|
|
6 months    [                                        ]
|           [                                        ]
|
12 months   [                                        ]
|
|
18 months   [                                        ]
|
|
24 months
|
|
30 months   [                                        ]
```

Further reading

Bee, H. (2000) *The Developing Child* (9th edn). New York: Longman. This well-known developmental psychology textbook has an excellent chapter on the development of language.

Owens, R.E. (2001) *Language Development: an introduction* (5th edn). Needham Heights, Mass: Allyn and Bacon. This is a detailed but accessible book on language development. It covers the whole process of language development thoroughly and deals with a variety of other aspects such as bilingualism and language disorders in children.

The American Speech Language Hearing Association has an excellent online site that deals with language development, bilingualism and activities to encourage speech and language development in children: www.asha.org/speech/development

5

Theories of language acquisition

Introduction
Environmental theories of language acquisition
Nativist theories of language acquisition
Social interactionist theories of language acquisition
Summary
Review exercise

Introduction

The previous chapter described some studies of language development. The striking feature of these studies is the speed that children acquire both words and grammar. Children largely master the very complex skill of using language by the age of 5 or 6. In just a few years children learn an enormous number of words and the intricacies of how to put these words into meaningful sentences, and they can produce and understand novel sentences. However, as Messer (2000, p.138) points out, 'there still remains controversy about how children are able to acquire language so quickly, given the immaturity of their other cognitive abilities and the lack of formal tuition'. The theories of how children acquire language fall into three main categories:

1. Environmental theories of language acquisition that stress the role of learning of both words and grammar.

2. Nativist theories of language acquisition which suggest that we have an innate ability to recognise and use grammar.
3. Social interactionist theories of language acquisition that stress the social nature of language and its importance in interaction with others.

Environmental theories of language acquisition

Learning theory

One of the earliest psychological theories of how children acquire language was put forward by the behaviourist Skinner (1957). Skinner believed that all behaviour is learned by operant or classical conditioning, described in detail in another book in the series (*The Determinants of Animal Behaviour*, Cartwright, 2002). In his book, '*Verbal Behavior*' Skinner argued that language is simply another form of behaviour that can be learned like any other behaviour. He believes the basis of all learning is *reinforcement*. A reinforcement is something that strengthens a behaviour and makes it more likely to occur again. For example, if a hungry rat gets a food pellet after pushing a lever it is more likely to push the lever again. The food pellet acts as a reinforcement. Many studies have shown that attention and praise are powerful reinforcements for infants and children. Skinner suggested that when infants initially produce babbling sounds they are reinforced by the attention of adults. This reinforcement makes it more likely that the infant repeats the sounds. Skinner also empha-sised the role of selective reinforcement and behaviour-shaping in language learning. Behaviour-shaping is the gradual moulding of a simple behaviour into a complex behaviour. For example, Skinner taught pigeons to hold small bats in their beaks and play ping-pong by shaping a simple pecking behaviour. He suggested that parents use a similar process to gradually shape the sounds the infant makes into words. Thus the sound 'da' might be reinforced initially but later the child will only get attention from their father if they say 'dada'. Skinner calls the verbal labels used to name objects or events *tacts*.

The shaping process continues as the child gets reinforced for putting words together. For example, a young child may be given a drink after saying 'juice' but later is more likely to get the desired response by saying 'more juice'. Later still the child is required to produce sentences that become closer approximations of the adult version. Skinner calls verbal behaviours that result in reinforcement in this way *mands* and they tend to be in the form of requests or commands. Skinner also discusses the role of *echoic responses* (or imitation) in language learning. Children may learn to name things by imitating adults if the echoic response is reinforced. Thus if an adult points to a duck and says 'duck' and the child imitates this they are likely to be reinforced with a positive comment. However, if the child then points to a pigeon and says 'duck' the parental response will tend to be negative ('no, that's not a duck'). Skinner suggests that echoic responses can also be used in learning how to combine words. For example, a child may imitate the sentence 'Do you want teddy?' by saying 'Want teddy'. If the child is then given the toy it reinforces the sequence and the child is likely to repeat it when requesting the toy in the future.

Evaluation of Skinner's theory

Although Skinner's theory seemed to be a plausible and logical account of language acquisition it soon became apparent that there are alot of problems with it. Firstly, there is little evidence that parents systematically reinforce language (or verbal behaviour) in children (Chomsky, 1959). Chomsky points out that learning language through reinforcement would be a slow process that would require careful shaping. However, children learn language quickly without parents teaching words and sentence structure carefully. Most evidence suggests that parents ignore grammatical errors in young children and respond to the meaning of what they say (e.g. Brown and Hanlon, 1970). Thus if a child had seen some sheep but reports 'I saw some cows' they would usually be corrected. However, if they report 'I saw some sheeps' they would not be corrected despite the grammatical error. Even if speech is corrected it tends to have little effect. If parents try to correct pronunciation or grammar children often still produce their version (Harley, 2001). This suggests that learning theory cannot explain how children acquire grammar.

Chomsky also questioned whether the learning theory could explain the universality of language development. If learning were responsible for language acquisition there would be more variation in language development between and within different cultures. The learning theory also appears to have difficulty in accounting for the creativity of language. Children quickly learn to understand and produce sentences they have never heard before.

The role of imitation in language learning has also been questioned for a number of reasons (Owens, 2001). Children acquire correct grammar despite being exposed to lots of incomplete sentences and ungrammatical speech. Much of the speech between adults is in the form of fragments of sentences, poor grammar and repetitions yet children learn to use the correct form. The use of overregularisation (see p.44) suggests that children acquire language by applying rules rather than by imitation. If a child uses the word 'goed' as the past tense of 'go' this indicates that they are applying a rule ('ed' indicates past tense) rather than using imitation (adults do not say 'goed'). Finally, when children do imitate adult speech they tend to convert it to a form similar to their own spontaneous speech. Thus if a young child imitated the adult sentence 'I am playing with the toys', s/he would change it to the telegraphic version 'play toy'.

Despite the problems in explaining the development of language Skinner's theory does seem to be relevant in explaining how children learn the meaning of some individual words. Owens (2001) points out that the processes that Skinner identified (reinforcement and shaping of words) are used in speech therapy programmes for children with language difficulties and are effective in promoting the use of language. It is therefore possible that this process also occurs in normal language learning.

Child-directed speech ('motherese')

Later environmental accounts of language acquisition have suggested that there is a special form of language that parents use to communicate with children and that this facilitates learning. This has been called *motherese,* but since fathers and other adults also use it the term **child-directed speech** is often used (Snow, 1994). Child-directed speech is a simplified form of speech in which adults alter both the presentation and content to make the speech accessible to the child. The speech is presented slower and in a higher pitch than adult speech and the phrases are segmented to make them clearer. Sentences are short, with simple forms of grammar and simple, restricted vocabulary. In addition there tends to be a lot of repetition in the speech (e.g. 'Where is teddy? Here is teddy'). The type of child-directed speech changes as the child gets older and both the presentation and content become more complex to reflect the linguistic abilities of the child.

Child-directed speech appears in nearly all cultures and it seems that children are drawn to it. For example Werker *et al.* (1994) found that English and Chinese infants preferred to listen to child-directed speech regardless of whether it was spoken in English or Cantonese. This suggests it has some important function and leads to questions about its role in language acquisition (e.g. Bee, 2000). It is possible that drawing attention to this simple form of language allows the child to learn basic language structure. Once they have mastered the basics the child-directed speech becomes more complex and the child can then learn new, more elaborate structures.

Messer (2000) claims there is evidence that it is a particular part of child-directed speech, called *adult expansions*, which helps in the development of grammar. Adult expansions are used to give feedback about correct grammar when a child uses incorrect grammar. Saxton (1997) has proposed the contrast theory of negative input which suggests that children learn from the juxtaposition of their incorrect form and an adult's correct form because of the contrast. He uses several examples to illustrate the idea (p.145):

a) Child: He SHOOTED the fish.
   Adult: He SHOT the fish!
b) Child: Do you know how Big Foot was BORNED?
   Adult: No, how was he BORN?

Thus there is an immediate contrast between the incorrect and correct version and Saxton believes it is this that helps the child learn. Consequently, each time adults use expansions they are helping to teach grammar to the child. (See Key Research Summaries, Article 2, p.112 for a full discussion of Saxton's theory).

Evaluation of the role of child-directed speech

There have been some studies that have found a correlation between children's language development and the degree of simplification of mother's speech, but other studies have failed to replicate this (Messer, 1999). Furthermore, even if such a correlation were to exist it does not show that child-directed speech *caused* better development. There are problems with the idea that child-directed speech allows children to acquire language. One is that, although child-directed speech appears in most cultures, it is not universal. For example, Pye (1986) could not detect the use of any child-directed speech in the Mayan culture. There is also evidence that the style of child-directed speech varies greatly across cultures (Lieven, 1994). Since all children acquire language in a similar way regardless of culture this suggests that child-directed speech is not responsible for acquisition. Many researches have concluded that child-directed speech may be useful in developing language but that it is not *necessary* for language to develop (e.g. Bee, 2000). However, Snow (1995) argues that although some features of child-directed speech are not found in all cultures it has yet to be established whether any culture fails to modify adult speech at all to communicate to children.

The idea that children learn rules of language because of immediate feedback is supported by research into language using **connectionist networks**. Connectionist networks (or neural networks) are computer simulations that are designed to mimic the way information is processed in the brain. These programs respond to feedback and in effect learn from the feedback. Although they are very simple it has been shown that connectionist networks are capable of learning grammatical rules such as past tenses of verbs (Shanks, 1993). The networks not only learned the past tenses of regular verbs (e.g. add 'ed' to the verb) but irregular forms as well (e.g. 'went' not 'goed'). It has been suggested that the network learned irregular forms quickly because they tend to be verbs that are often used (Messer, 2000). Since these relatively simple networks are capable of learning grammatical rules through feedback it is possible that children (who are much more complex than networks) can also learn language from feedback.

Progress exercise

Try to arrange a time with family or friends when you can unobtrusively observe parent/s talking to a young child. Note whether there is any evidence of:

1. Systematic reinforcement of the child's language.
2. The adult/s using child-directed speech.
3. The adult/s providing feedback using adult expansions.

Do your observations support either of the environmental theories?

Nativist theories of language acquisition

Nativist theories argue that the ability to acquire language is innate and that children are programmed to learn language. The most prominent supporter of this view is Chomsky (1957, 1959, 1965), who argues that only some form of pre-programming can explain the speed with which children learn the complex skill of using language and the similarity of language acquisition across cultures (as described in the previous chapter). Chomsky noted that all human languages share certain features (i.e. they all have nouns and verbs), which are called 'linguistic universals'. He suggested we have an innate mechanism called the **language acquisition device** (LAD) that allows children to identify the grammar of the language to which they are exposed by picking out the linguistic universals. He believed that only something like the LAD could explain how children are able to learn correct grammar from the fragments of sentences and incorrect grammar they hear. Chomsky believes that the LAD is unique to humans and that no other animal uses language or can be trained to use language.

Chomsky also proposed that there are two levels to every sentence. One level is simply the words we speak or hear that make the sentence: the **surface structure**. The other level is the meaning of the sentence: the **deep structure**. When we speak we have to transform an idea or thought into a sentence (e.g. from deep to surface), but when we listen we have to transform the sentence into a meaningful idea (e.g. from surface to deep). Sentences are changed from one structure to another by using **transformational grammar**. Sentences can have very different surface structures yet the same deep structure. For example,

The dog chased the man
The man was chased by the dog

are different in surface structure but conjure up the same image or deep structure. On the other hand, one surface structure can have a variety of deep structures (e.g. hearing someone say 'I can see a man eating fish' has very different connotations, depending on whether you are walking past a restaurant or swimming in the ocean!). Chomsky believes that ability to transform sentences from deep to surface or vice versa (transformational grammar) is a major function of the LAD and is innate.

Over the past twenty years or so Chomsky has expanded on his original ideas to produce a theory that recognises the complexity of language (e.g. 1986, 1995). In the government and binding theory he suggests that, although there are linguistic universals, languages vary in a number of parameters (hence the alternative name 'principles and parameter theory', or PPT). Language acquisition consists of learning the correct version of any parameter from hearing the adult speech. Messer (2000) illustrates this by comparing word order in English and Japanese. Sentences in English are usually in subject–verb–object order but in Japanese they are subject–object–verb order. Thus any child exposed to English speech would have the word-order parameter set for subject–verb–object but a child exposed to Japanese would have the same parameter set for subject–object–verb.

Evaluation of Chomsky's theory

Chomsky's theory has been the most influential theory of language acquisition and has dominated psycholinguistics for the past forty years. There is evidence from a variety of sources that supports the theory. For example, the process of language acquisition discussed in Chapter 4 is very similar in all cultures. When a process is similar in every culture regardless of environment this suggests it is maturational (i.e. biologically based). Furthermore, all languages share features (the linguistic universals) and this suggests that there may be a common underlying feature such as the LAD.

Lenneberg (1967) is a strong proponent of the idea that language has some form of biological basis. He has suggested the *critical period hypothesis*, which consists of two strands. One idea is that certain events must happen within a critical time period for normal development. Specifically children must be exposed to a language before puberty (10–12) or they will not be able to learn to use language. The other is that certain features of language (and other aspects of development) can only happen when the critical period is reached. There is evidence for both these ideas. The first idea is difficult to test since nearly every child is exposed to language well before puberty. However, there are a few cases of children who, because of severe deprivation, have not been exposed to much language until they were older. Perhaps the most famous case is that of Genie who from the age of 20 months until she was nearly 14 heard very little language (Curtiss, 1977). Genie's father disliked noise and there was very little speech in the house and no radio or TV. Genie was kept isolated in a small room and virtually her only human contact was when her mother fed her each day. Unsurprisingly, when she was taken into care she had very few linguistic skills although she could understand a few words. Despite the intensive training she has been given Genie never learned to speak fluently and could not master many of the grammatical skills that most children pick up so easily. She did learn to say words and could produce sentences but it was as if she was speaking a second language poorly. However, the fact that she learned to use language at all suggests that there is not a fixed critical period for language learning; rather there is a sensitive period (Harley, 2001).

Lenneberg's second idea was that language development is a maturational process akin to motor development and that certain behaviours can only be shown when critical stages have been reached. He observed that certain motor developments seem to correspond to language developments (e.g. crawling–babbling, standing–first words, etc.). In children where development was delayed the delay affected both motor and language skills. This again suggests a maturational not environmental process. This is further supported by studies of language acquisition in deaf children. Deaf children seem to learn sign language in similar stages as children learning spoken language. Goldin-Meadow and Feldman (1977) studied four deaf children who had not been taught sign language but who nevertheless communicated initially by using one sign then a combination of two signs etc. This suggests some need or drive to use language.

It is also argued that only something like the LAD can explain how children can learn a language from the poverty of what they hear. Despite hearing fragments of speech and ungrammatical speech children still manage to pick out the correct use of grammar. Chomsky argues that this is because of the LAD. Finally, phenomena such as overregularisation suggests that rules are at the heart of language acquisition, and it is these rules which are the centre of Chomsky's theory.

However, the emphasis on the rules of grammar (or syntax) can be regarded as one of the problems of Chomsky's theory since it ignores the use of language to communicate (or pragmatics). As we will see in the next section some researchers feel that it is the need to communicate that is the driving force in language acquisition. There is evidence that children do not learn language merely by exposure but by *interacting with people using* language (see social interactionist theories p.61). Owens (2001) points out that sentences can be syntactically correct but meaningless or nonsensical. However, children do not use grammatically correct meaningless sentences but sentences that communicate meaning. The nativist account of language acquisition also largely ignores the importance of environment. However, the environment clearly is important in the learning of word meaning, accent and the grammar of the language. There is growing evidence that children do not learn 'rules' of grammar but, as environmental theories suggest, gradually learn to use different verbs, adjectives, etc. (e.g. Tomasello, 1992; Pine and Lieven, 1997). Tomasello (1992) has suggested that children learn 'verb islands' which represent the most commonly used verbs but that the rules of these verbs are not applied to others. One of the problems of the government and binding theory is explaining bilingualism or second-language learning. If language acquisition consists of setting the parameters of language how do children manage to learn two languages with different parameters?

The studies of language learning using connectionist networks (see p.56) has also challenged Chomsky's claim that language learning is so complex that there must be a unique innate mechanism to enable children to do so. Connectionist networks are designed to mimic the way humans learn and are able to learn seemingly complex 'rules' of grammar. The networks are trained by giving feedback about whether its responses are correct or incorrect. Messer (2000) suggests the connectionist network research into language challenges Chomsky's theory in three ways. Firstly, the way the networks learn is not specialised for language but can be applied to non-linguistic learning. Secondly, the networks do not require any specific 'innate' knowledge to learn rules of grammar. Finally, although the network behaves as if it is using rules no linguistic rules were pre-programmed.

Chomsky's claim that language is unique to humans because only humans inherit a LAD is subject to intense debate that centres on definitions of 'language' (for a discussion of this debate see the chapter on animal language in another book in this series: *Animal Cognition*, Lund, 2002). However, a number of studies suggest that some animals such as chimpanzees and bonobos are capable of learning some aspects of language (e.g. Savage-Rumbaugh and Brakke, 1996).

Social interactionist theories of language acquisition

Language is not an abstract skill but, during childhood, develops into our primary means of communication and social interaction. The social interactionist theories of language believe that it is the need to communicate and interact with others that is the driving force behind language acquisition. In contrast to the nativists the social interaction theorists do not believe that mere exposure to language is sufficient to acquire it but that it is a skill learned by interacting with others. They concentrate on the pragmatics of language not the syntax. Bruner (1983) describes a **language acquisition socialization system** (LASS) which, in contrast to the LAD, focuses on the social nature of language. There is evidence that the skills of interacting with others precede both the comprehension and production of words or language. For example, one vital aspect of using language to communicate is turn-taking. We cannot hold a conversation if everyone talks at the same time. A lot of research suggests that infants learn to use 'turn-taking' in their interactions with adults long before they start using speech (Harley, 2001).

Evaluation of social interaction theory

Harley (2001) believes that few people would disagree with the central idea of the social interactionists; that is, that effective language acquisition must take place in a social setting. There is also evidence that this is the case. For example, Messer (2000, p.140) notes that when the main source about language is television 'children make little or no progress with the language they hear'. This is illustrated by the case of 'Jim' who, until the age of 3, only heard language on television because his parents were deaf (Sachs *et al.*, 1981). Jim had learned to use words but both his articulation and grammar were very poor. One of the first rules that most children learn is the use of an 's' to make a plural, but Jim still could not do this at the age of 3. Television exposes children to language but children do not learn well from it because it does not interact with them. Another source of evidence for the social interactionist theory is the language development of twins. The language acquisition of twins is often slower than average until about school age when they catch up. One reason for this could be that, although they hear the same amount of language as any other child, less of it is used in interacting with each individual twin (Messer, 2000).

There are a number of problems with the social interactionist theory. Firstly, the style of interaction between infants and adults varies across cultures and if language acquisition depends on this interaction there should be differences between cultures. However, as the nativists note, many aspects of language acquisition seem to be universal. Secondly, this approach has been criticised because there is a tendency to be vague about exactly how social interactions influence language acquisition (e.g. Harley, 2001).

Summary

There are a number of different theories of how children acquire language, but they fall into three main types: environmental, nativist and social interactionist theories. The environmental theories concentrate on the role of learning in language acquisition. Skinner proposed that reinforcement and behaviour shaping of the child's vocalisations could explain acquisition of language (or verbal behaviour). However, parents do not seem to reinforce children's speech selectively and this theory does not seem to explain the universality and creativity of language. The simplified version of speech adults use to children (or child-directed speech) may help in the acquisition of language but since it does not appear in all cultures it is unlikely to be responsible for language development. Nativist theories, such as Chomsky's, emphasise the role of innate mechanisms in language acquisition. Chomsky suggests that humans have a language acquisition device (LAD) that enables children to learn any language simply by being exposed to it. This is supported by the existence of linguistic universals and the universal nature of language acquisition. However, the theory concentrates on the syntax of language and ignores its social and communicative aspects. The social interaction theory stresses the importance of language in communication and suggests that language is acquired through using language whilst interacting with others. However, this account of language acquisition has problems in explaining why children from all cultures learn language in a similar way.

Review the three approaches discussed in this chapter and complete the following table:

	Central concept	Main evidence	Main limitation
Environmental theory (Skinner)			
Nativist theory (Chomsky)			
Interactionist theory (Bruner)			

Review exercise

Further reading

Owens, R.E. (2001) *Language Development: an introduction* (5th edn). Needham Heights, Mass: Allyn and Bacon. This book covers the theories of language development clearly and thoroughly.

Harley, T.A. (2001) *The Psychology of Language: from data to theory* (2nd edn). Hove: Psychology Press. A comprehensive book on all aspects of language, including theories of development.

6

Problem-solving

Introduction
Types of problems
Gestalt approach
Information-processing approach
Information processing and 'insight'
Use of analogy in problem-solving
Problem-solving in everyday life
Summary
Review exercise

Introduction

The need to solve problems is a common feature of our lives. There are many different types of problem, ranging from simple to complex and trivial to life threatening. A well-known example of a complex, life-threatening problem arose in the space flight of Apollo 13. During the journey towards the moon, some 200,000 miles from the earth, there was an explosion and the spacecraft sustained extensive damage. This was announced to mission control in the famously understated message 'Houston, we've had a problem.' The problem was how to turn the spacecraft around and return to the earth whilst sustaining the lives of the three astronauts aboard with limited power, water and oxygen. Most of us do not have to deal with such dramatic problems, but nevertheless we deal with problems daily. You may be faced with the problem of how to get home when you have missed the bus, how to get in touch with someone when you have lost their telephone number, how to help a friend who is unhappy, how to produce an excellent psychology essay, etc.

Since the problems people deal with are so diverse we are faced with the question: 'What is a problem?' Garnham and Oakhill (1994, p.217) suggest that 'Problems arise when people do not see immediately how to get from where they are (starting state) to where they want to be (their goal state).' This description introduces a number of essential elements of problems. Every problem has a **start state** (or initial state) and this is the position you begin with. For the crew of Apollo 13 this was being in deep space in a damaged spacecraft, but if you are trying to write an essay the start state may be sitting with a blank sheet of paper in front of you. The **goal state** is the state you want to achieve (returning safely to the earth or producing a grade A essay). Something is only a problem if we do *not know* how to get from the start state to the goal state, since if we can immediately see how to achieve the goal state it is not a problem. For each problem there are different types of processes or actions that enable us to get from one state to another; these are called **operators**. For the crew of Apollo 13 the operators involved changes to navigation plans, conserving water, living in the lunar module, etc. Another feature of many problems is that the process of going from the start state to the goal state cannot be achieved in one stage – you have to pass through a number of inter-mediate stages to reach the goal state (see p.75).

This chapter initially looks at problems that are designed by psychologists and studied in laboratory settings. These problems are usually clearly defined and the start state, goal state and operators are specified. However, since most problems in real life are not well defined the chapter ends by examining problem-solving in real life.

Types of problems

There are many types of problems faced by people, both in laboratory studies and in everyday life, and many researchers find it useful to try to categorise them. For example, Robertson (2001) suggests that problems could be categorised according to the type of solution that is required. One way problems differ is in the level of knowledge needed to solve them. Some problems do not require much prior knowledge to solve them (for example, the nine-dot problem on p.68); these are called *knowledge-lean*. However, other problems are *knowledge-rich;* that is, the solution requires prior knowledge (e.g. if I were to ask you to translate an article from a German newspaper you would need knowledge of German). The strategies used to find solutions to knowledge-lean problems can often be applied to a variety of problems and they are therefore *domain-general*. However, the strategies used to find the solutions to knowledge-rich problems are usually only useful to the particular type of problem and are therefore *domain-specific*. Problems can also differ in how well they are defined. When problems are *well-defined* the start state and the goal state are clearly identified. Furthermore, in well-defined problems the actions (or operators) which are allowed or prohibited are also known (see, for example, the Hobbits and Orcs problem on page 72). In *ill-defined* problems one or more of the parameters (start state, goal state, operators, prohibited operators) are not known.

Problems can also be categorised as adversarial or non-adversarial. **Non-adversarial problems** are problems in which an individual or a group is required to find the solution to a problem but there is no competition with others. These problems are typically puzzles of some sort and are usually well defined but knowledge-lean and domain-general. **Adversarial problems** involve competition with other people and the goal is to defeat your opponent(s). These problems are typically games of some sort (such as chess) and usually knowledge-rich, domain-specific and less well defined than puzzles (although the rules or operators are explicit in adversarial problems the goal is beat the opponent, not a specific state).

The following discussion focuses on various approaches to understanding non-adversarial problems before examining problem-solving in real life.

(Readers interested in adversarial problems should refer to the 'Further reading' section at the end of the chapter and to Box 6.1 on p.79.)

Before studying the findings of research into problem-solving it is worth looking at some of the problems used by psychologists. Try solving them and note down the thoughts you have whilst thinking about each problem, or if you have a friend to work with act as 'solver' and 'note-taker' on alternate problems.

1. *Nine-dot problem (see Figure 6.1)*

Draw four straight lines that go through all nine dots without taking the pen from the page or retracing your route.

Figure 6.1 **The nine-dot problem**

2. *Candle problem (based on Duncker, 1945)*

First, collect together a candle, a box of matches and a box of drawing pins. The problem is how to attach the candle to a wall in such a way that it will not drip wax on the floor when lit.

3. *The water jar problem (based on Luchins, 1942)*

Imagine you have three different-sized jars that can measure a precise volume of water. Jar A can hold 9 litres, jar B can hold 42 litres and jar C can hold 6 litres. The problem is how to measure 21 litres accurately.

(The solutions are on pp.123–124 should you become too frustrated by any problem!)

Gestalt approach

Some of the earliest psychological research into problem-solving was performed by Gestalt psychologists at the beginning of the twentieth century. The Gestalt approach originated in the study of perception and one of the basic ideas was that people perceive whole objects (rather than adding up the parts of an object). This approach was extended to problem-solving and the Gestalt psychologists believed that problem-solving required an understanding of the overall structure of a problem rather than focusing on each element of the problem in turn. Gestalt psychologists typically studied problem-solving by using verbal protocols (see p.6). They were more interested in the process of problem-solving than the solution, and verbal protocols are a way of studying the process. From these studies of human problem-solving the Gestalt psychologists believed that solutions came from an **insight** into the problem and occurred when participants **restructured** the problem. Insight occurs when the participants are suddenly aware of the answer (i.e. the participant does not gradually work towards a solution, rather it appears in a flash). If you managed to solve the nine-dot problem in the progress exercise above you may have experienced insight. Once you realise that the lines do not have to be within the square formed by the dots the problem has been restructured.

The concepts of insight and restructuring are illustrated by the Gestalt 'two-string' problem set by Maier (1931). In this problem participants were faced with two strings hanging from the ceiling and their task was to tie the two strings together. However, the strings were set too far apart for the participants to reach both at once and if they held one string they could not reach the other. Maier left a number of objects lying on the floor and one solution to the problem was to use the pliers. If the pliers were tied to the end of one of the strings it acted as a pendulum and the string could be swung back and forth. The participant could then hold the other string and catch the swinging string. Some participants solved the problem quickly, and showed insight since they claimed that the solution suddenly came to them. Other participants needed help in restructuring the problem and Maier found that if he 'accidentally' brushed against the string to set it swinging participants who had been struggling suddenly saw the answer. The swinging string had enabled them to restructure the problem (although many claimed they were unaware of the hint).

Gestalt approach and thinking

The Gestalt studies led to the idea that there are different types of thinking that can be applied to solving problems. Wertheimer (1945) distinguished between **reproductive thinking** and **productive thinking**. Reproductive thinking involves using previous experience of problem-solving to solve new ones. For example, if you were to learn a mathematical rule while solving one problem you could use this rule when faced with a similar problem. Whilst this approach can be useful it can also lead to problems since people do not notice the structure of the problem and may not see other simpler solutions. Reproductive thinking may be therefore 'structurally blind' (Robertson, 2001) and may result in a failure to find a solution or in an inefficient solution. Productive thinking, on the other hand, involves an understanding of the underlying structure of the problem and is more likely to lead to a restructuring of the problem and an insight into the solution.

Wertheimer (1945) illustrated the difference in the types of thinking by teaching two groups of students how to calculate the area of a parallelogram in two different ways. One group were taught to use a mathematical procedure that the area = length of base x perpendicular height (or h x b). The other group was taught to understand the formula by restructuring the parallelogram to form a simpler shape, a rectangle (if you cut one end off the parallelogram and place it at the other end you can form a rectangle). Both groups of students were able to calculate the area of parallelograms equally well. However, when faced with other unusual shapes such as a circular segment missing at one end and a circular segment added at the other end the students who had learned the mathematical procedure could not calculate its area. They were using reproductive thinking and the formula they had learned did not help with the new problem. The participants who had been encouraged to focus on the structure of the original problem were able to calculate the area of other unusual shapes. Using productive thinking they were able to restructure other problems to find solutions.

Reproductive thinking and problem-solving

The Gestalt psychologists argued that there are a number of possible negative effects of past experience and reproductive thinking such as

problem-solving set and **functional fixedness**. Problem-solving set occurs when participants learn to solve a series of problems in a specific manner. The solution then becomes a habit (or a mental set) which is used even if a simpler solution is possible. For example, Luchins (1942) gave participants a number of variations of the water jar problem (see p.68). The control group of participants was asked to solve a series of problems that required different types of solution. The 'set' group was asked to solve a series of problems that all required a similar solution. All the participants were then presented with a critical test that could either be solved simply or by using a more complex solution based on that the set group had used. The control group tended to use the simple solution, but the set group tended to use the complex solution they had learned on previous trials. Functional fixedness occurs when we focus on the normal function of an object and therefore fail to appreciate that it could have alternative uses. This is illustrated in Duncker's (1945) candle problem (see p.68). Many participants fail to solve the problem because they perceive the box containing the matches as a matchbox only and fail to recognise that it may have other uses – as a candleholder, for example.

Evaluation of Gestalt approach

The Gestalt approach has been very influential in the study of problem-solving. The basic method they used to study problems – verbal protocols – is still used in most research even now. Many of the problems they studied are still provoking debate some six decades after they were first used. Eysenck and Keane (2000) point out that the information-processing approach (see p.73) owes much to Gestalt ideas such as productive thinking.

However, despite the appeal of the Gestalt explanations of problem-solving there are a number of problems with the approach. Most of these stem from the vagueness of the concepts which the Gestalt psychologists used. For example, the notions of restructuring and insight are not clearly defined and there is little explanation as to why they occur or fail to occur. Both concepts seem to be intuitively accurate descriptions of solving problems but do not explain the underlying processes.

Try solving the following problems and, as with the previous exercise, record your thoughts as you try to solve them.

1. *Tower of Hanoi (see Figure 6.2)*

   Move the rings on peg A so that they form an identical arrangement on peg C. Only one peg can be moved at a time and a larger ring cannot be placed on top of a smaller ring. (NB: This is a simple version of this problem; the more rings the more difficult it becomes!)

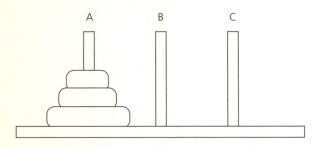

   Figure 6.2 Tower of Hanoi

2. *Hobbits and Orcs (see Figure 6.3)*

   Imagine there are three Hobbits and three Orcs on one side of a fast-flowing river. Everybody in the party needs to cross the river but there is only one canoe and this can only carry two at a time. Getting the whole party across is complicated by the aggressive nature of the Orcs because if the Orcs outnumber the Hobbits on either bank they will kill those Hobbits. This includes any Orcs that come to the shore in the canoe. Hobbits, on the other hand, are peace-loving creatures and it does not matter if they outnumber the Orcs. The strong current means that at least one Hobbit or Orc has to be in the canoe to make the crossing in either direction. What is the least number of crossings with the canoe that need to be made to get the whole party safely across?

Start State

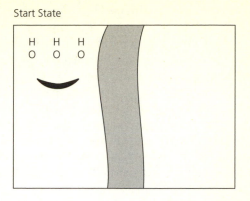

Goal State

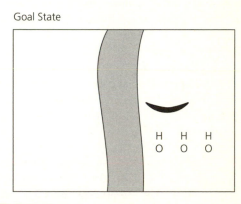

Figure 6.3 **The Hobbits and Orcs problem**

(The solutions are on pp.124–128.)

Information-processing approach

Much of the information-processing approach to problem-solving
stems from the work of Newell and Simon (1972). Their book *Human
Problem Solving* describes and explains many of the key concepts
of the information-processing approach. One of these key concepts
is that, like computers, humans can only solve problems by analysing
and manipulating information. In trying to solve a problem we have
to use a number of sequential stages to reach the solution. Sometimes

these stages do not lead to a solution and we have to go back a few stages and try again. In the Tower of Hanoi problem on p.72, for example, one might think about putting the smaller ring on peg B and the middle ring on peg C before realising that the largest ring could not go on either peg. Newell and Simon called this type of mental representation of the problem the '**problem space**'. Once we know the initial state – and the operators we can use – the problem space is like the mental path we take to the goal state. Sometimes this will involve going down the wrong path and we have to go back to try another route. In a problem like that of the Hobbits and Orcs (p.72) the possibilities that can exist in the problem space increase with each successive move.

Newell and Simon (1972) used these ideas to develop a computer program called the **General Problem Solver** (GPS). The GPS was designed as a model of human problem-solving and was based on studies of people solving problems. One important aspect of the GPS was the strategy it was programmed to use for solving problems. Based on their earlier work, Newell and Simon (1972) outlined two distinct problem-solving strategies. One strategy for solving problems is to use **algorithms**. This algorithmic method involves a systematic search of all the possible solutions to a problem until the correct answer is identified. For example, if you are asked to solve the following anagram, 'unqietos', you can find the solution by systematically examining all the possible solutions. So the next combination you try may be 'unqietso' and the next 'unqiesto', etc. Eventually a systematic search of the 40,320 possible combinations of these letters would reveal one or more recognisable words. However, most research suggests that humans do not use this approach often because a search of *all* of the possible solutions takes too much time and effort. The alternative approach is to use rules of thumb that act as short cuts and enable a selective search for the most likely solutions. These rules of thumb are called **heuristics**, and are solutions that often work although they do not guarantee finding the correct solution. In the example of the anagram above there is a 'q' and a 'u', and we know that they go together in English; we also know that 'ion' is a common combination. These short cuts, or heuristics, would probably lead to the solution – in this case, 'question'. However, this solution is not guaranteed. We could use the heuristic that 'un' is a common beginning to words and by focusing on this fail to find the correct solution.

The heuristic strategy Newell and Simon built into the GPS was **means-ends analysis**. Means-ends analysis was a heuristic device that was observed in human problem-solving. When faced with a complex problem we cannot usually find a solution that requires one operation (i.e. we cannot go straight from the initial state to the goal state); rather, we have to break the problem up into a series of *sub-goals* that we tackle one at a time. Each sub-goal is used to reduce the difference between the initial state and the goal state. Of course setting a goal does not guarantee that it will be achieved, and each sub-goal (or 'end') requires an operator (or 'means') to achieve it: hence the name 'means-ends analysis'. In human problem-solving requiring a series of moves, like the Hobbits and Orcs problem, participants do not make moves steadily from the initial state to the goal state but pause before making groups of moves (e.g. Greeno, 1974). This seems to reflect sub-goaling: when the participant solves one sub-goal they make a series of moves before considering how to achieve the next sub-goal.

The computer simulation of the means-ends analysis that Newell and Simon (1972) built into the GPS successfully mimicked the behaviour of humans on a number of problems. For example, Thomas (1974) found that human participants have difficulty with the Hobbits and Orcs problem because the most successful solution at one point requires two creatures to return across the river. This does not seem to reduce the difference between the initial state and goal state but to increase it, and participants are reluctant to make this move. (Look back at your notes for the previous exercise; did you get stuck after move 5? Move 6 is the one which requires one Orc and one Hobbit to go back to the bank that they started on.) The GPS successfully mimicked this and the manner in which participants solved other problems

Evaluation of the information-processing approach

Newell and Simon's work on the information-processing approach has had an enormous impact on the understanding of problem-solving. They put forward a theory that introduced a variety of key concepts in the area, such as the use of heuristics in problem-solving and a large body of research that examined the topic. Eysenck and Keane (2000, p.407) claim that the theory 'makes substantial and fundamental contributions to cognitive theory and to our understanding of people's problem-solving abilities'.

Despite this Newell and Simon eventually abandoned the GPS because it only applied to certain types of problem – specifically well-defined problems. However, most of the problems the people solve tend to be ill-defined (see p.67). In addition, people are often faced with several problems that they have to deal with at once, but the GPS was designed to solve problems one at a time (Matlin, 2002). Nevertheless the concepts that Newell and Simon introduced are still at the core of research and theory into problem-solving.

Information processing and 'insight'

The information-processing approach seems to work well on problems that require step-by-step solutions (such as the Hobbits and Orcs problem) where a sequence of moves are needed to achieve the goal state. However, this approach seems to have some difficulty in explaining the types of problems studied by the Gestalt psychologists, problems whose solutions require 'insight' (such as the nine-dot problem). Knoblich *et al.* (2001) suggest that such problems pose a double challenge for the information-processing approach. Firstly, why do people fail to solve these problems for some time when most have the ability to do so? Secondly, what is it that allows people to break the impasse and solve the problem? People do not receive any new information yet the answer frequently appears suddenly. This raises the question of whether information processing can explain problems that seem to require insight.

Some researchers have suggested that there is a distinction between insight and non-insight problems. For example, Metcalfe and Wiebe (1987) investigated participants' 'feeling-of-knowing' (or FOK) as they attempted to solve both insight and non-insight problems. FOK is the individual participant's estimate of how close they are to solving a problem. During non-insight problems the participant's FOK *gradually* increased from very low (e.g. definitely do not know the answer) to high (e.g. getting very close to an answer). However, when attempting to solve insight problems the participant's FOK remained low until just before the answer was found. This suggests that there is a distinction between the two types of problem.

Nevertheless, there have been a number of information-processing accounts of insight such as Kaplan and Simon (1990) or MacGregor *et al.* (2001). Robertson (2001) points out that the accounts tend to have many features in common and that these features, such as searching through a problem space or retrieving relevant operators from memory, are found in accounts of non-insight problem-solving. For example, Kaplan and Simon (1990) suggest that insight-type problems require a search for an appropriate problem space (see p.74) whereas non-insight problems require a search through a problem space for a solution. More recently, MacGregor *et al.* (2001) have proposed a computational model of participants' performance on the nine-dot and similar problems. The model has a number of components which are typical of information-processing models, such as searching the problem and selecting moves that maximise the number of dots with a line through them (e.g. a difference-reduction heuristic). The model seems to predict a participant's performance on the problems well and to explain why the problem cannot be solved initially and how the solution is reached. Robertson (2001) notes that 'MacGregor et al. have succeeded in building a detailed process model of success and failure on abstractly defined problems.'

Use of analogy in problem-solving

Another type of heuristic device for solving problems is to adapt solutions for similar problems from the past. This type of heuristic is the use of **analogy**. For example, if I find a solution to the problem of how to cut five equal portions of a pie I can adapt that solution if faced with the problem of cutting five equal portions of a pizza. Analogies clearly have the potential to be a very useful problem-solving heuristic – but do people use them? One way of studying the use of analogies is to present participants with a problem together with the solution and then present them with an analogous problem. The participant's performance can then be studied to assess whether they use the analogous solution or not. One example of this approach is a study by Gick and Holyoak (1980). They used an analogous problem to the 'inoperable tumour problem' that was originally posed by Duncker (1945). In the original problem participants are told of a patient who has an inoperable tumour that can only be cured by a strong dose of radiation. However, although weak doses of radiation do not harm normal tissue the strong dose required to cure the tumour would not only destroy the tumour but the surrounding tissue as well. The solution to this problem is to aim a number of weak beams of radiation at the tumour from different angles. These weak beams do not harm the normal tissue but combine to form a strong concentration on the tumour. The analogous problem introduced by Gick and Holyoak (1980) involved a general trying to capture a fortress that can be approached by a number of roads. However, each of these roads is mined and any large group of troops would detonate the mines, although a small group would not. The solution is analogous to the solution to the inoperable-tumour problem since a number of small groups of troops can be sent down each road to form a large force at the fortress. Gick and Holyoak found that merely presenting the general's problem did not improve participants' performance on the inoperable-tumour problem, but if participants were instructed to use the analogy they performed better.

There seem to be a number of factors that affect whether analogies are used or not. One factor that has been widely investigated is the degree of similarity of the analogous problems. These studies suggest that participants tend to focus on the superficial content of the problem (or the **surface features**) rather than the underlying similarities (or the **structural features**) or the principles of the problem and solution (Matlin, 2002). For example, if given two problems with similar surface features, such as treating an inoperable brain tumour and treating an inoperable lung tumour, participants can transfer the solution well. However, participants are less good at transferring solutions between two problems with different surface structures but with the same essential structural features (such as the inoperable tumour and the general's problem). Matlin (2002) also notes that solutions to problems are often context-bound. Thus a solution learned in one context is not easily transferred to another context or setting.

Although a number of studies suggest most participants do not use analogous problem-solving well there are a number of methods for increasing the effective use of analogies. Matlin (2002) outlines four factors that seem to improve analogous problem-solving. She notes that the use of analogies increases if:

1. Participants are given explicit instructions to compare problems.

2. Participants are shown several structurally similar problems before being given a similar one.
3. Participants are given a hint that the solution to an earlier problem may be helpful.
4. Participants study the structure of the problem rather than the surface features.

However, these conditions do not usually exist in everyday life because when we encounter a problem we are not told to compare it to previous problems, nor are we guided to concentrate on the structural rather than surface features, etc. Therefore there is doubt about the relevance of analogies in solving real-life problems.

Box 6.1. Adversarial problems: game playing and expertise

In the studies of non-adversarial puzzle solving the problems used required novel solutions and were not based on previous knowledge (knowledge-lean problems). However, many problems people face are knowledge-rich and require practice or training to develop expertise in a topic. If my car failed to start I would not be able to fix it because I have no knowledge of how an engine works. I would have to call a mechanic who has knowledge of car engines and expertise in diagnosing and fixing engine problems. The study of adversarial problems has allowed researchers to investigate the development of expertise and to compare the difference in strategies between novices and experts. Another feature of adversarial problems is that, like many real problems, the goal state is not well defined. In a game such as chess the goal state is to beat the opponent, but there is no set position for any of the chess pieces. Many of the studies of both adversarial problems and expertise have concentrated on chess for a number of reasons. Firstly, chess potentially presents a very complex problem and it is estimated that from an opening board there are 10^{120} possibilities (Garnham and Oakhill, 1994). Secondly, performance in chess can be evaluated, either by who wins or by using the agreed rating scale to measure the ability of any player (from novice to grandmaster).

Much of the work on performance in chess stems from DeGroot (1965) who studied the difference between grandmasters and good players. He found that players considered a relatively limited amount of moves, and that,

---

surprisingly, the grandmasters did not consider more moves than the less-expert players. However, the grandmasters made quicker moves that were judged to be better. The limited consideration of alternatives shown by grandmasters is in contrast to computer chess programs which tend to consider a huge number of alternatives. For example, Deep Blue searches about 90 billion alternatives each move. This is clearly not possible for a human player, yet until recently computer 'players' could not beat the best human players. This suggests that human players must have some other means to achieve expertise rather than a detailed analysis of every alternative move and countermove. DeGroot proposed that experts differed in their knowledge of board positions. Grandmasters have a great deal of experience of playing chess and tend to study the games of other experts. This knowledge enables them to discount irrelevant moves and concentrate on a few likely ones.

Other studies have shown that it is not just knowledge and memory that differentiates experts from non-experts – they also differ in the way information is used. Garnham and Oakhill (1994, p.226) point out that experts' knowledge 'is organised differently from that of novices, and it enables them to encode new information more efficiently'. For example, Chase and Simon (1973) asked three chess players of differing ability to replicate the position of pieces on a board. They recorded the timing of each glance at the board and how many pieces were placed on the second board after each glance. They found that the expert player recognised 'chunks' of the board quicker and was able to recognise more pieces with each glance than the novice could.

The study of games like chess has led to a great interest in experts, and it is an important topic in cognitive psychology. Apart from increasing our understanding of how people become expert the studies have led to the development of computer simulations of experts or 'expert systems'. These studies have not been limited to chess or other adversarial games but to expertise in a wide range of human activity, including medicine, physics and writing. Although the nature of expertise may differ there seem to be some common features of experts. Robertson (2001) discusses a number of these features; among the most important are:

1. Experts tend to be expert in one area (or domain).
2. Experts are able to categorise problems quicker than novices.

3. Experts are more efficient in perceiving chunks of information than novices.
4. Experts have efficient strategies for using long-term memory for dealing with tasks whereas novices tend to rely on short-term memory (which is limited).

Problem-solving in everyday life

Most of the problems described so far in this chapter have been well-defined problems that have been studied in controlled settings. However, the problems we encounter in everyday life are not well defined and often we have only a vague notion of the goal state and a poor understanding of the possible processes to achieve it. Furthermore, we frequently need to find solutions whilst dealing with various sources of distraction. This raises the question of the relevance of the formal studies of problem-solving. There is a danger that these studies only show how people solve abstract problems in psychology laboratories and have little to do with real life. An obvious way of addressing this issue would be to study 'normal' problem-solving in a natural setting such as home or work. However, there have been surprisingly few studies of this kind. Garnham and Oakhill (1994) have suggested a number of reasons for this. Firstly, unlike the laboratory-based studies, there is not a clearly recognised method for studying natural problem-solving. Secondly, there are problems in understanding how the participants interpret the problem and their interpretation may be very different to that of the researcher. Finally, in contrast to the laboratory-based problems, real-life problems seldom have a correct or ideal answer and it is therefore difficult to assess the participant's performance.

Despite these problems there are a few studies of real-life problem-solving. For example, Carraher *et al.* (1985) studied the mathematical abilities of children selling goods in Brazilian street markets. They found that, despite a lack of formal education, the children solved complex mental arithmetic problems which related to their usual activities when they were tested on the streets. Carraher *et al.* (1985) also found that the children often used unusual methods to solve mental arithmetic problems. However, when they were moved to a more formal setting and asked to solve similar problems they did less well. It seems that, as with the more controlled studies, the ability to solve problems is not easily transferred from one context to another. Scribner (1984) looked at everyday problem-solving by studying different groups of workers in a dairy. As with the previous study, Scribner found that people used innovative and efficient methods for solving problems. One worker, who had to prepare cases and part cases for delivery, claimed not to count out the orders but to visualise the numbers needed. The workers at the dairy were better at finding optimal solutions to loading the deliveries than people, such as students, who had formal training in arithmetic.

Garnham and Oakhill (1994) suggest that findings like these show that people are more adaptable and inventive in real life than in formal laboratory studies. Perhaps when problems are real and solutions bring tangible rewards (such as less walking backwards and forwards to prepare a delivery) people are more motivated to find solutions, or perhaps real-life problems have more relevance. Whatever the reason, Garnham and Oakhill (1994, p.271) claim the findings of the real-life problem-solving 'indicate a need to be cautious in drawing conclusions about ordinary thinking from the results of laboratory studies of how people solve contrived problems'.

Summary

Problems are a common aspect of our daily lives and they occur when we cannot immediately perceive the way to goal state. One of the earliest approaches to study problem-solving was the Gestalt approach. This approach emphasises the way problems are looked at as a whole and concentrated on insight methods of problem-solving. They suggested that solutions required restructuring of the problem. Although the Gestalt approach provided some useful methods of studying problems it did not provide an adequate explanation of problem-solving. A more recent approach to problem-solving is the information-processing approach, typified by the work of Newell and Simon (1972). They developed a computer program called the General Problem Solver (GPS) which used heuristic methods of solving problems. Heuristics are rules of thumb that can be used as short cuts to find solutions, but they do not always provide the correct solution (as opposed to algorithms that do find the correct solution in a systematic way, although this can be slow). The heuristic used in the GPS was 'means-ends analysis'. Solving problems with means-ends analysis involves breaking down the problem into sub-goals which help reduce the difference between the initial state and the goal state. Another heuristic that could be used for solving problems is the use of analogies. If a person learns or is shown the solution to one problem they should in theory be able to use this solution to help solve a similar problem. However, this heuristic is only used when the surface features of the problems are similar or if participants are given instructions to pay attention to the structural features. A number of studies of problem-solving in real life have suggested that people are inventive and adaptable and have led to doubts about the relevance of the laboratory-based studies.

Write a brief description of the following approaches to the study of problem-solving:

1. Gestalt approach.
2. Information-processing approach.
3. Use of analogies.

List one positive and one negative criticism of each approach.

Review exercise

Further reading

Garnham, A. and Oakhill, J. (1994) *Thinking and Reasoning*. Oxford: Blackwell. This is an advanced textbook that has a good chapter on problem-solving (non-adversarial problems). It also has an interesting chapter on game playing and expertise (adversarial problems).

Robertson, S.I. (2001) *Problem-Solving*. Hove: Psychology Press. This book is aimed at undergraduates, but it is also very accessible to A-level students. It explains ideas very clearly and is written in an engaging and witty style.

7

Decision-making

Introduction
The heuristics and biases approach to judgements
Other factors that influence judgements
Evaluation of the heuristics and biases approach
Theories of decision-making
Summary
Review exercise

Introduction

Human lives tend to be complicated and we are faced with a multitude of choices daily. Many of these are trivial, such as whether to have another cup of coffee or not; others can be life changing or life threatening, such as whether to end a relationship or where to cross a road. Sometimes decision-making requires a simple choice of one of two possible actions, such as whether to take a taxi or a bus. Even such a simple choice involves weighing the costs and benefits. However, making decisions often involves a more complex mix of weighing probabilities, personal desires and personal beliefs. Thus, given the same choices, one person may risk a great deal because of political or religious beliefs but another may be unwilling to take any risk. Sometimes the 'logical' decision may be resisted because of factors such as tradition or emotional ties. For example, it might make financial sense to trade in an old car that is costing a lot in repairs but a person may decide not to do so because they have become attached to it.

Garnham and Oakhill (1994) point out that decisions involving probability judgements fall into two categories: decision-making under risk and decision-making under uncertainty. Decision-making under risk occurs when the probabilities of outcomes are known. For example, if you throw a dice there is a 1 in 6 chance of getting any number. Decision-making under uncertainty occurs when the probabilities of outcomes are not known. Most of the examples in this chapter are concerned with decision-making under risk and these depend on probability judgements of risk and rewards. We have to decide, given a possible reward, whether a risk is worth taking. This chapter starts by looking at some of the heuristics used to make these judgements, then moves on to discuss theories of decision-making.

The heuristics and biases approach to judgements

Making decisions can be difficult since we are required to weigh up various possibilities, often with critical pieces of information missing. The judgement we form in order to make decisions therefore often requires the use of short cuts or heuristics (see p.74). Heuristics can be invaluable since they enable decisions to be made quickly and, often, accurately. The study of heuristics in making judgements has been dominated by two researchers, Kahneman and Tversky. They have suggested that a limited number of heuristics are used in making judgements and, although these heuristics usually lead to accurate decisions, they can also lead to errors and biases. Hence this approach has been called the *heuristics and biases approach* (Tversky and Kahneman, 1974; Kahneman and Tversky, 1996). Kahneman and Tversky tend to focus on how heuristics lead to errors in thinking about probability. Three of the heuristics – representativeness, availability, and anchoring and adjusting – are discussed below.

The representativeness heuristic

The **representativeness heuristic** is used when a person, object or event is judged to be a member of a class or group because there is a resemblance to a prototype or stereotype of that class or group. It is therefore based on similarity and often ignores other pertinent information such as relative size of the group or class. For example, if I described someone as competitive and very fit and then ask whether that person was more likely to be an Olympic 100-metre runner or a librarian you would probably choose the former. This is because the description of someone as competitive and fit seems representative of an athlete. However, this judgement ignores the fact that there are a lot more librarians than Olympic 100-metre runners.

The use of the representativeness heuristic was illustrated in a study by Kahneman and Tversky (1973) when they asked participants to judge the occupation of someone based on a description. The participants were told the description was chosen at random from a set of a hundred descriptions of either lawyers or engineers. Half the participants were told there were descriptions of seventy lawyers and thirty engineers and the other half were told there were thirty lawyers and seventy engineers. The description given to the participants conformed to the stereotype of an engineer but not to a lawyer. The participants judged that there was a 90 per cent chance that the person was an engineer *regardless* of the other information they had been given (i.e. they ignored the 70:30 or 30:70 ratio of engineer to lawyer). Thus the decision was influenced by the similarity (representativeness) of the description to an engineer alone. This tendency to ignore information about how often something occurs in the population (or base rate) is called the **base-rate fallacy**.

The representativeness heuristic has been used to explain the **conjunction fallacy**. This occurs when people believe that the conjunction of two events is more likely than either one of the two events occurring alone. This was illustrated in a study by Tversky and Kahneman (1983, p.297), who gave participants the following description:

> Linda is 31 years old, single, outspoken and very bright. She majored in Philosophy. As a student she was deeply concerned with issues of discrimination and social justice, and also participated in antinuclear demonstrations.

The participants were then given a number of options which they were asked to rank from most likely to least likely. These options included statements such as 'Linda is a bank teller', 'Linda is a teacher', 'Linda is active in the feminist movement' and 'Linda is a bank teller and is active in the feminist movement'. Interestingly, most participants rated 'Linda is a bank teller and is active in the feminist movement' as being more likely than 'Linda is a bank teller'. Kahneman and Tversky argue that logically this *cannot* be the case since not all bank tellers are active in the feminist movement. As there are more bank tellers than bank tellers active in the feminist movement it is more likely that Linda is a bank teller. However, the description contains elements that seem to make Linda representative of the feminist movement thus leading to the conclusion that she is both a bank teller and a feminist.

The use of representativeness can also lead to misjudgements of small samples. A sample is often judged as more likely if it resembles the population as a whole. For example, if people are given the following sequences of coin tosses:

THHTHT   or   TTTTTT

and asked to judge which is more likely they tend to choose the first because it seems more representative. This is because in a large sample of coin tosses we would expect half heads and half tails. However, both sequences are *equally likely* since there are sixty-four possible sequences with six tosses and each sequence above represents one of those. When people are presented with a sequence such as TTTTTT and asked whether heads or tails is more likely next time they tend to judge heads more likely (Garnham and Oakhill, 1994). However, the odds of the coin falling as a head or a tail remains the same at 50:50 *regardless* of what has happened before. This is similar to the *gambler's fallacy,* which is the belief that a sequence of losses must be followed by a win.

Although the representiveness heuristic can lead to misjudgements in many cases it is a sensible heuristic to use. If something shows many of the characteristics of a class of objects it probably belongs to that class (or as Kunda, 1999, puts it 'anything that looks like a duck, walks like a duck, and quacks like a duck is most likely a duck').

Read through the following two lists quickly and then decide whether there are more women or men in each list. (Based on Kahneman and Tversky, 1973.)

List A	List B
David Beckham	Jennifer Lopez
Jane Austen	John Steinbeck
Anna Ford	David Niven
Brad Pitt	Kate Moss
Katharine Hepburn	Richard Briers
Robbie Williams	Victoria Beckham
Cherie Booth	Peter Mandelson
Enid Blyton	Lewis Carroll
Tony Blair	Margaret Thatcher
Ewan McGregor	Kylie Minogue
Juliette Stevenson	John Ford
John Travolta	Julia Roberts
Iris Murdoch	Joseph Conrad
Angela Rippon	Keith Moon
Jonathan Ross	Naomi Campbell
Charlotte Rampling	Tommy Cooper
Barbara Stanwyck	Robert Taylor
George Bush	Britney Spears
Tom Cruise	Kate Winslet

Now count the names in each list. Was your snap judgement correct? If not, think of a reason why each list seemed distorted (see p.90 for an explanation).

Progress exercise

The availability heuristic

The second heuristic described by Tversky and Kahneman (1973) is the **availability heuristic**. They suggest that some judgements of the probability of an event, or that something will have certain characteristics, are based on the availability of information from memory. If people can think of a number of examples they tend to overestimate the probability, but if they cannot think of examples they tend to underestimate probability. The effect of availability was shown by Tversky and Kahneman (1973) when they asked participants whether letters such as K or R were more common as the first letter or third letter in English words. Most participants estimate that the letters are more common as the initial letter of words, but in fact both are much more common as the third letter. Tversky and Kahneman believe that the availability heuristic explains the error because it is easier to bring examples of words beginning with K or R to mind than examples when they are the third letters. The availability heuristic may explain why some highly publicised events are judged as more common than they actually are. People tend to overestimate the number of murders in Britain; perhaps this is because, although they are rare, they are headline news.

Matlin (2002) describes two influences on the availability heuristic: recency and familiarity. Recency refers to the tendency for memories to fade; therefore more recent examples of an event are more readily available. For example, if people are asked to estimate the number of deaths on the railways following a major rail accident they tend to give a higher estimate than after a period of no accidents. This influence of recency may have applications in therapy. MacLeod and Campbell (1992) found that if people were asked to remember pleasant events they tended to believe that it was more probable that pleasant events would occur in the future (they became more optimistic). However, if they were asked to remember unpleasant events they tended to be more pessimistic and judged that unpleasant events were more likely. The availability heuristic can also influence some people's perception of politicians. For example, Haddock (2002) asked participants to think of either positive or negative characteristics of Tony Blair and found that this influenced the perception of him in those participants with little interest in politics. However, there was less influence in the participants who did have an interest in politics, presumably because they were not influenced by the availability of recent memories.

Familiarity refers to the amount of contact a person has with a subject. For example, a person who has met many people who are divorced will tend to give a greater estimate of divorce rates than a person who has little contact with divorcees (Matlin, 2002). The influence of familiarity was shown in a study by Kahneman and Tversky (1973) in which they read participants a list of thirty-nine names. The list either consisted of nineteen famous women and twenty less famous men or nineteen famous men and twenty less famous women. Participants were asked which sex was more common in the list and tended to give the incorrect judgement that the famous sex was more common than the less famous sex. Presumably the familiarity of the nineteen famous names misled participants into judging that there were more of that sex than the twenty less famous names (review your answers for the progress exercise on p.89).

Kahneman and Tversky (1982) have suggested that there is a particular type of availability heuristic called the *simulation heuristic*. The availability heuristic is based on the ease of recall of actual examples, such as words or accidents. However, the simulation heuristic is based on how easy it is to imagine examples. If people find it easy to imagine that an event may happen they tend to judge it as more likely than an event they cannot imagine. For example, I have a friend who every year places a bet that Port Vale will win the FA Cup. As an avid supporter he imagines (or simulates) a successful cup run each year and this leads him to judge that Port Vale may win. Most other football supporters would find it difficult to imagine that Port Vale could win the cup and would not make the same judgement.

The anchoring and adjustment heuristic

The third heuristic proposed by Tversky and Kahneman (1974) is the **anchoring and adjustment heuristic**. They suggested that when making estimates or judging probability people often take an initial value, an anchor, and then adjust it. For example, if you are negotiating the price of a second-hand car the price given by the vendor acts as an anchor. However, studies into judgement suggest there is a tendency to under-adjust if the anchor is inaccurate. Therefore if the anchor is inaccurate the final estimate or judgement tends to be inaccurate. If the anchor is very high people will adjust down, but only a little; conversely, if the anchor is very low people adjust up – but again it is an underestimate. For example, Tversky and Kahneman (1974) gave participants a random number between 0 and 100 and then asked them if that figure was higher or lower than the percentage of African countries in the United Nations. They then asked the participants to give an estimate of the percentage of African countries in the United Nations. When given an initial figure of ten participants gave an average estimate of 25 per cent but if the initial figure was sixty-five the average estimate was 45 per cent. They seemed to use the initial figure as an anchor even though they knew it was random.

Matlin (2002) notes that the anchor and adjustment heuristic is not restricted to artificial estimates of numbers but has been applied to a variety of real situations such as risk assessment and estimates of property values. It has even been applied to aspects of social psychology such as judgements of people. For example, we may use stereotypes about particular groups (e.g. accountants) to anchor a person and even if the person does not fit the stereotype we are reluctant to adjust our view about them (Kunda, 1999). The heuristic can be difficult to avoid and many examiners are aware of it when they are the second person to mark a script or piece of coursework. There is a danger that the first mark acts as an anchor and influences the mark given by the second examiner. Many examiners re-marking or moderating marks avoid looking at mark sheets for this reason.

There is some debate about whether the anchor and adjustment is a different type of heuristic from availability. The presence of an anchor obviously provides a value that is available and this may influence the estimates given by participants. However, the availability heuristic does not explain why the estimates are under-adjusted (Manktelow, 1999).

Progress exercise

Explain how:

1. The availability heuristic may affect a doctor's diagnosis of a rare disease.
2. The anchoring and adjustment heuristic may affect the decision of what price to offer for a house.

Other factors that influence judgements

Framing effect

One strong influence on judgements and risk-taking behaviour is the way the problem is presented to participants; this is known as the

framing effect. The framing effect has been shown in numerous studies, but its influence tends to be caused by one of two factors: the wording of the problem or the background context of the problem (Matlin, 2002).

A lot of research has shown the influence of the wording of a problem on decision-making. For example, Tversky and Kahneman (1981) gave different groups of participants two versions of the 'Asian disease problem'. These are shown as problems 1 and 2 below:

Problem 1
In problem 1 participants were told that there was going to be an outbreak of an unusual Asian disease in the United States which was expected to kill 600 people. There were two possible programmes to deal with the disease: A and B. If programme A were used 200 people would be saved. If programme B were used there would be a one-third probability that 600 people would be saved and a two-thirds probability that no one would be saved.

Problem 2
In problem 2 participants were given the same background information as for problem 1 (an Asian disease was expected to kill 600 people), but the two programmes (A or B) were phrased differently. If programme A were used 400 people would die. If programme B were used there would be a one-third probability that nobody would die and a two-thirds probability that everybody would die.

In both problems the deep structure is the same – only the surface structure differs (see p.78). Problem 1 is positively framed (it emphasises the number of lives saved), whereas problem 2 is negatively framed (it emphasises the number of lives lost). Statistically all four answers produce the *same* average outcome: 200 people are saved and 400 die. However, the framing of the question produced very different decisions. When presented with problem 1, 72 per cent of the participants chose programme A. However, when presented with problem 2, 78 per cent of the participants chose programme B. It seems that if programme A is presented as a sure gain participants avoid taking a risk (programme B) but if it is presented as a sure loss participants are willing to gamble on saving more lives. In this instance the wording of the problem had a strong influence on risk-taking behaviour.

Another factor that influences the framing effect is the background information that is provided. For example, Tversky and Kahneman (1981) asked participants to imagine that they were buying goods in a store that cost $140 in total (one item for $125 and another for $15). They were then asked to imagine that another store sold the same items for $5 less and asked whether they would be willing to travel to that store to save the $5. Tversky and Kahneman (1981) found that the decision depended upon the item that was $5 cheaper. If the $15 item was $5 cheaper participants were more likely to decide to go to the other store than if it was the $125 item. However, in both cases the saving and the inconvenience are the same! It seems that participants regard a saving of $5 on a $15 item as being more than a saving on a $125 item. In a similar example Tversky and Kahneman (1981) asked participants whether they would buy another ticket costing $10 if they arrived at the theatre and found they had lost their original ticket. Alternatively, participants were asked whether they would buy a ticket costing $10 if they arrived at the theatre and found they had lost $10. Participants were more likely to buy a ticket if they had lost $10 than if they had lost the original ticket, even though the financial loss was the same. In both these examples the decision taken is influenced by the background to the problem rather than the financial consequences.

Although these studies might be criticised as being artificial and lacking in ecological validity a number of studies have shown that the framing effect can influence consumer behaviour. For example, Johnson (1987) found that people are more likely to buy minced beef if it is described as '80 per cent lean' than if it is described as '20 per cent fat'. Advertising is essentially framing the information about the product to try to influence the consumer to buy it.

Overconfidence

It seems that people tend to be **overconfident** about their decisions (i.e. they are more confident about the accuracy of their decision than their actual performance warrants). This is typically studied by asking participants to choose one of two answers to a question and then asking them to rate their confidence in the answer. A rating of 50 per cent would be chance level (i.e. the participant has no idea which answer is correct) and a rating of 100 per cent would indicate that the participant was absolutely sure that they had chosen the correct answer. Most studies show that when participants report 100 per cent confidence in their answer they are actually correct about 80 per cent of the time (e.g. Lichtenstein *et al.*, 1982). The level of overconfidence is influenced by a number of factors such as the type of question (being lowest on easy questions and highest on 'trick' questions) and gender (males tend to be more overconfident in their decisions than females).

As with the studies of the framing effect these studies could be criticised as being artificial. However, the concept of overconfidence in decisions has been found to apply to real-life situations, including military decisions about whether to launch missiles and students' decisions about when to begin assignments (Matlin, 2002).

Hindsight bias

Most people are aware that answers seem obvious when they are told the answer; this tendency leads to the **hindsight bias**. This is the tendency to be more confident about the predicting accuracy of an answer once the answer is known. For example, Fischhoff (1977) gave one group of participants a number of general knowledge questions and asked them to choose the correct answers and then assign a probability of the answers being correct. Another group was given the correct answers and was then asked to assign a probability that they would have given those answers. The second group gave higher confidence levels than the first. In hindsight they were confident that they would have given the right answers. The hindsight bias explains the tendency of people to say 'I knew that' when you tell them the answer to a question or problem.

Evaluation of the heuristics and biases approach

The heuristics and biases approach introduced by Kahneman and Tversky has dominated the study of judgement and decision-making during the past three decades. The research methods they used and the concept that heuristics form the basis of most human judgements and decisions permeate throughout the literature in this area. Their theory has been used to explain a number of different types of research findings and, as Manktelow (1999, p.175) notes, 'one of the strengths of Kahneman and Tversky's heuristic theory is that it can predict results in a wide range of tasks'. Eysenck and Keane (2000) point out that the theory has generated much research and is relevant to a number of important practical applications of psychology. For example, the approach has been applied to decision-making in business, and Maule and Hodgkinson (2002) describe how heuristics are used in strategic decisions in corporations and how biases such as the framing bias can distort business decisions. This explains why Kahneman was awarded a Nobel Prize in 2002, not for Psychology, but for Economic Science. The concepts of heuristics and biases have even been used to explain belief in the paranormal (Blackmore and Troscianko, 1985). People who believe in paranormal occurrences tend to be more prone to errors of judgement about the probability of events happening and therefore do not believe that events happen by chance.

However, there is not total agreement with this approach and an alternative view of decision-making has emerged which is largely associated with Gigerenzer and his colleagues (e.g. Gigerenzer, 1991, 1996). Matlin (2002) characterises the two different positions as the pessimistic and optimistic views of decision-making. Kahneman and Tversky's approach is the pessimistic view since it tends to emphasise the errors and seeming irrationality of human decision-making. Gigerenzer's approach is the optimistic view since it emphasises the accuracy of decision-making when people are given better information about factors such as base rate. One of the main differences in the two approaches is that Kahneman and Tversky tend to present people with information expressed as probabilities whereas Gigerenzer tends to present information expressed as frequencies. Gigerenzer (1996) believes that people are better able to deal with information expressed as frequencies. He also argues that Kahneman and Tversky tend to focus on a statistical analysis of problems without considering the influence of real-life experiences. Furthermore, he suggests that Kahneman and Tversky do not explain how or when the various heuristics are used. In other words they provide a description of heuristics which do not explain a full understanding of the processes involved.

The debate between these two views is an intense one and is well illustrated by articles in which the two positions are argued (see Research Articles 3 and 4 – Kahneman and Tversky, 1996 and Gigerenzer, 1996 on pp.114–117). The outcome of the debate may well influence the future direction of research into human judgement and decision-making.

Briefly describe the following three heuristics:

1. Representativeness.
2. Availability.
3. Anchoring and adjustment.

Indicate how each can lead to biases in judgement.

Theories of decision-making

The discussion in this chapter so far has concentrated on the judgements of probability people use in order to make decisions. Some decisions are made solely on the basis of such judgements (e.g. the decision to take an umbrella because it is judged that rain is probable). However, many decisions are not made on the basis of judgement of probability alone because a lot of decisions are also influenced by needs and desires. As Manktelow (1999, p.191) notes 'decision making . . . fundamentally concerns combining information about probability with information about desires and interests'. So, for example, the decision of whether to revise or go out with friends is based both on judgements about how likely it is you will pass the exam *and* on how much you *want* to pass (and how much you want to go out!). There are a number of theories of how people use various types of information to make decisions but the basis for most is the subjective expected utility theory.

Subjective expected utility (SEU) theory

The subjective expected utility (SEU) theory suggests that when making decisions people weigh up the expected utility of an outcome against the probability that the outcome will happen. In this context expected utility is something that is useful or desirable, such as more money or better health. The notion of expected utility was first proposed by von Neumann and Morgenstern (1944), who suggested that decision-making is like gambling and we bet on the best probable outcome. This idea was modified by Savage (1954), who argues that the concept of utility is subjective since what is desirable for one person might not be for another. Thus a first prize of a case of wine in a raffle might have high expected utility for one person but low for another whose religion prohibits alcohol. For this reason Savage suggested that the idea of subjective expected utility was preferable. In its simplest form SEU can be calculated by multiplying the probability of an outcome by its subjective utility:

SEU = (probability of an outcome) × (subjective utility)

Thus an outcome may have a low probability of happening but have a high subjective utility and therefore a high SEU. This may explain why millions of people buy lottery tickets each week despite knowing that the probability of winning is very low – the subjective utility of a win is very high.

The SEU theory is built on the idea that if people follow a number of principles (or axioms) they will maximise their expected utility. Some of the more important principles are:

1. People's preferences are well ordered. So if there are two outcomes, A and B, then either A is preferred to B, B is preferred to A or neither is preferred (indifference).
2. Following on from the first principle the second suggests that people's preferences are transitive. This means that if someone prefers A to B and prefers B to C then A is preferred to C.
3. The third principle is the independence principle. This is that if there is a factor that remains the same no matter what the decision is then it should not influence the decision. For example, if there were two alternative routes to a friend's house and both took 20 minutes then time should not be a factor in deciding the route.
4. Finally there is the sure-thing principle. This suggests that if A is preferred to B in every situation then A should be preferred even when the situation is not known. For example, if you prefer route A to your friend's house whether it is sunny or raining you should choose route A even when you do not know the weather.

Evaluation

These principles seem very straightforward and may even seem like common sense. However, the SEU has been challenged because a variety of studies have shown that people do not follow these principles. For example, there are a number of 'paradoxes', such as the Allias and Ellsberg paradoxes, which show that people do not always use the principle of independence. There are even studies that show people do not always follow the sure-thing principle. Tversky and Shafir (1992) asked participants to imagine they had taken a qualifying exam and now had the opportunity of a desirable five-day holiday in Hawaii at a very low price. However, this was a special offer which ended the next day. Participants were asked whether they would buy the holiday, put down a deposit to secure the holiday at the discount price, or not take the holiday. Participants were placed in one of three conditions: (a) they knew they had passed the exam, (b) they knew they had failed the exam, or (c) they would not know the result until after the offer had expired. The decision made by the first two groups were approximately the same, and about 55 per cent opted for buying the holiday and 30 per cent opted to put down a deposit. Thus the majority opted to buy the holiday whether they had passed or failed. According to the sure-thing principle the group that did not know the result should be similar. However, this group were different as only 32 per cent opted to buy the holiday and 61 per cent chose to place a deposit (i.e. they did not follow the sure-thing principle). This study suggests that when people do not know what state they are in they tend to avoid making decisions. Tversky and Shafir labelled this the *disjunction effect*.

Another problem with the SEU is that it does not explain the various studies of the framing effect (see p.92). In these studies the context of the problem, or the way the problem is phrased, affects the decision that participants make. However, analysis of the various outcomes shows them to be the same utility. Thus the subjective expected utility is the same but the decisions are not.

Prospect theory

The prospect theory, proposed by Kahneman and Tversky (1979), is essentially a modification of the SEU that attempts to explain the framing effect and apparent paradoxes in decision-making. It starts with the same central assumptions as the SEU, such as regarding decisions as if they are gambles and that people gamble on achieving the best outcome. It also shares the assumption that decisions are made on the basis of judgements about probability and subjective utility. However, the prospect theory differs in a number of important respects. Firstly, it suggests that people do not make decisions based on absolute gains and losses but rather assess expected utility relative to *reference points*. A reference point is usually the state a person is in prior to the decision and gains and losses are assessed relative to this point. This idea seems to explain the framing effect. A common aspect of the framing effect is risk-aversion if there is already a gain, but risk-seeking if there is already a loss (Garnham and Oakhill, 1994). For instance, in the Asian disease example on p.93 in problem 1 participants typically chose programme A because from this reference point there are 200 people saved so why risk killing them all? However, in problem 2, participants typically chose option B because from this reference point 400 people will die so why not taking a chance on saving everyone. The absolute values of how many survive or die in all options do not vary but the outcome relative to the reference point does.

The second major difference between the SEU and the prospect theory is that the SEU assumes there is a linear relationship between value and utility but the prospect theory does not. The prospect theory suggests there is a non-linear S-shaped relationship between value and utility. This suggests that it is the gains and losses nearest to the reference point that are the most important. So, for example, most people would enjoy winning £10 yet the subjective utility of winning £1,000 would be even higher. However, the subjective utility of winning £1,010 would not be noticeably higher than the subjective utility of winning £1,000.

Evaluation

The prospect theory is much better at describing how people make decisions than the SEU. It can also explain some of the paradoxes and effects of framing that could not be explained by the SEU. The prospect theory has been described as 'the most influential contemporary descriptive theory of decision making' (Manktelow, 1999, p.204). However, it does not deal with all aspects of decision-making – the role of emotions, for example. Some theories, such as the regret theory

(Loomes and Sugden, 1982), focus on the influence of anticipated emotions in decision-making (e.g. would the regret of making a decision that was wrong outweigh the rejoicing if the decision was right?).

Summary

Kahneman and Tversky argue that there are a number of heuristics involved in making judgements and that, although these heuristics often work, they can lead to biases in judgement; this is known as the heuristics and biases approach. The representativeness heuristic is the tendency to judge that something belongs to a group or class based on its similarity to a prototype of the group or class. This can lead to the base-rate fallacy and the conjunction fallacy. The availability heuristic is the tendency to make judgements based on examples available from memory rather than reality. It seems to be influenced by both familiarity and recency. Kahneman and Tversky also described the anchoring and adjustment heuristic, which is the inclination to use given value as a starting point (anchor) and then to base judgements around it (adjustment). Other influences on decision-making include the framing effect. This is the influence of presentation of a problem on decisions and this can be affected by the wording of the question or the background information. Other studies have shown that people are inclined to be overconfident about the accuracy of their decisions and that this can have important consequences for decisions in real life. Another form of overconfidence is the hindsight bias. This is the tendency to be more confident about the ability to give an accurate answer when the correct answer is known. Kahneman and Tversky's approach has been very influential in the study of judgement and decision-making but has been criticised by Gigerenzer who has proposed an alternative, more 'optimistic' approach. There are a number of theories of decision-making but most are based to some extent on the subjective expected utility theory (SEU). The SEU suggests that decision-making is based on judgements of probability of an outcome and the subjective utility of the outcome. However, this theory fails to explain the framing effect or various studies that show paradoxes in the decisions participants made. The prospect theory suggests that decisions are made using reference points, not absolute values of gains and losses. This theory seems to explain some paradoxes and the framing effect more effectively.

1. What is meant by the 'heuristics and biases approach' to judgements?
2. Explain why understanding how people make judgements is central to understanding decisions.
3. What other major factor influences decision-making?
4. Explain why the prospect theory accounts for the framing effect better than the SEU.

Further reading

Manktelow, K. (1999) *Reasoning and Thinking*. Hove: Psychology Press. This is an undergraduate textbook but is written in a clear and engaging style that is accessible at A-level. Chapters 8 and 9 cover the material of this chapter in more depth.

Matlin, M.W. (2002) *Cognition* (5th edn). Orlando, Fla.: Harcourt, Inc. This is a general cognitive psychology textbook that has a good chapter on decision-making.

A recent issue of *The Psychologist* (2002, vol. 15, no. 2) focuses on judgement and decision-making. The articles cover a wide range of issues but the main focus is on how the ideas and theories discussed in this chapter have an impact on real-life decisions in business, on juries, etc.

8

Study Aids

IMPROVING YOUR ESSAY-WRITING SKILLS

At this point in the book you have acquired the knowledge necessary to tackle the exam yourself. Answering exam questions is a skill and in this chapter we hope to help you improve this skill. A common mistake that some students make is not providing the kind of evidence the examiner is looking for. Another is failing to answer the question properly, despite providing lots of information. Typically, a grade C answer is accurate and reasonably constructed, but has limited detail and commentary. To lift such an answer to an A or B grade may require no more than fuller detail, better use of material and a coherent organisation. By studying the essays below, and comments that follow, you can learn how to turn your grade C answers into grade A. Please note that marks given by the examiner in the practice essays should be used as a guide only and are not definitive. They represent the 'raw marks' given by an AQA examiner; that is, the marks the examiner would give to the examining board based on a total of 24 marks per question broken down into assessment objective 1 (description) and assessment objective 2 (evaluation). A table showing this scheme is in Appendix C of Paul Humphreys' *Exam Success in AQA(A) Psychology* in this series. They may not be the marks given on the examination certificate received ultimately by the student because all examining boards are required to use a common standardised system called the Uniform Mark Scale (UMS) which adjusts all raw scores to a single standard acceptable to all examining boards.

The essays are about the length a student would be able to write in 25–30 minutes (leaving you extra time for planning and checking). Each essay is followed by detailed comments about its strengths and weaknesses. The most common problems to look out for are:

- Students frequently fail to answer the actual question set, and present 'one they made earlier' (the *Blue Peter* answer).
- Many weak essays suffer from a lack of evaluation or commentary.
- On the other hand, sometimes students go too far in the other direction and their essays are all evaluation. Description is vital in demonstrating your knowledge and understanding of the selected topic.
- Don't write 'everything you know' in the hope that something will get credit. Excellence is displayed through selectivity, and therefore improvements can often be made by *removing* material which is irrelevant to the question set.

For more ideas on how to write good essays you should consult *Exam Success in AQA(A) Psychology* (in this series) by Paul Humphreys.

Practice essay 1

Describe and evaluate two theories of the relationship between language and thought. (24 marks)

Candidate's answer

The links between language and thought have been studied by philosophers for many years, but more recently, psychologists have joined the discussion. It is accepted that much thinking is done with words, but exactly what the relationship between language and thought is remains unclear. This essay will describe and evaluate two approaches because they offer opposite points of view.

The first approach – that language shapes thought – has been called the linguistic relativity hypothesis (LRH). It was first proposed by Sapir, a linguist, and Whorf, an anthropologist. The second approach suggests the opposite view that thought shapes language. This is a view held by Piaget who believed that language is dependent on cognitive development.

The LRH suggests that differences in the words we use actually mean differences not only in the way we think but also in the way we perceive the world. For example, the Hanuxoo people of the Philippines have ninety-two names for rice and, according to the LRH, this then means that they think about rice in very different ways from the average British person who is familiar with just a few categories of rice such as brown and white rice. The LRH suggests that vocabulary affects the way we think about our world; this also applies to the grammar we use. So, for example, the Hopi language makes no distinction between past, present and future, which for the average British person would make life impossible to contemplate. There are a number of versions of the LRH, such as the 'strong version' – which claims that language *determines* thought – and the 'weak version' – which claims that language *influences* thought.

All versions of the LRH are difficult to test as people are tested in their native languages, which means that instructions are translated but not always exactly. Nevertheless, there has been some support for the hypothesis, particularly the weak and cognitive versions but there is very little evidence for the strong version. The research of Carroll and Casagrande (1958) into the development of form and shape recognition between Navaho and English children is often used as evidence in support of the strong version, but it is ambiguous. Not all Navaho-speaking children developed form recognition earlier than the English children – which would have been expected. Criticisms of the strong version, and particularly of Whorf, have focused on the evidence he used, especially the lack of literal translations of words between languages.

Most research to date has been carried out on the weak version of the LRH which suggests that language influences thought and perception. For example, research using cross-cultural studies of colour perception has found that there are differences in the ways people of different cultures name and categorise colours (Rosch, 1973). However, this work was challenged by other research. For example, Berlin and Kay (1969) found that there is a systematic way in which different cultures categorise and code colour which follows a specific hierarchy and that this does not vary between cultures. If only two distinctions are made, then light and dark are the distinctions (black and white).

Red is the next distinction to be added, rising to eleven basic terms used to code colour regardless of culture. More recently, Davies (1998) has studied the colour task again and found that culture does influence colour boundaries (e.g. the boundary between what constitutes green or blue).

The second approach to be discussed is that thought shapes language. This is associated with the work of Piaget. He believed that in order to use words, a person must first think them. He believed that language development was a result of cognitive development. Although a child might use words before understanding them, Piaget believed that this was not using true language but egocentric speech.

There are several studies which support Piaget's approach. For example, Harley (2001) compared the cognitive development and language development of children when one of the functions was impaired. If cognitive development was impaired, then so too was language development. However, there are also studies which challenge this approach. For example, Bellugi *et al.* (1991) studied children with Williams' syndrome. This causes impairment of cognitive abilities but does not affect language skills.

In summary, it is clear that there are links between language and thought. However, at the present time, psychologists are not completely clear about exactly what and how those links are made and used.

Examiner's comment

This question clearly asks candidates to describe and evaluate *two* theories. A surprising number of candidates do not follow the injunctions of the question and discuss one or three/four theories. In such cases one theory would be classed as a partial answer and would gain a maximum of 16, and if three or more theories were discussed only the best two would gain credit. In this essay the candidate has discussed two since they have clearly signalled that the LRH has been regarded as *one* theory and therefore credit can be given for the different versions (strong and weak). (An alternative approach would be to argue that the different versions represent *different theories*. This would also be acceptable, but candidates should make this *explicit* to remove any doubts in the examiner's mind.) This essay has a good mix of description and evaluation but needs more elaboration, particularly on the theory that thought determines language, and is likely to gain 15 marks: 9 for description and 6 for evaluation.

This is a essay that demonstrates a good understanding of the topic and starts with two paragraphs that introduce the subject well. The next paragraph describes the LRH clearly and uses some good examples to illustrate the theory. The next two paragraphs present an evaluation of the LRH and use some good evidence, but not always well. For example, the candidate mentions the Carroll and Casagrande study to discuss the strong version of the LRH but does not explain why the study did or did not support the theory. Similarly, the candidate discusses a number of studies of perception and language but does not link these studies with the weak LRH well or mention the *implication* of the findings. (This is a common failing in exam essays; candidates present good evidence but do not discuss the conclusions or implications of the evidence.)

The next two paragraphs are a brief discussion of Piaget's theory that thought determines language. The first of these is a short but accurate description of the theory. However, the description would be better had it been more detailed. For example, the candidate could illustrate the theory with reference to the concept of conservation of mass or volume and could explain the meaning of the term 'egocentric speech'. The next paragraph is an evaluation of the theory, and the candidate uses some good evidence – but again the candidate does not use it effectively. For example, the Bellugi *et al.* study is summarised accurately but the candidate does not explain what implications this has for the theory.

Practice essay 2

Discuss research into decision-making in humans. (24 marks)

Candidate's answer

Human lives are complicated and full of difficulties. Each individual is faced with the task of making decisions every day of their lives, be it whether they should wear red or blue socks or more complicated ones. Everything we do depends on what decision we as humans make. These decisions that we make often depend on the risk and reward factor: we have to decide whether a risk is worth taking to get a reward.

Decision-making therefore often requires the use of short cuts or heuristics. This theory of heuristics has been developed by psychologists Kahneman and Tversky. They have suggested that a few heuristics are used in making decisions and these heuristics can lead to errors and biases.

Kahneman and Tversky described three heuristics: representative, availability, and anchoring and adjustment. The representative heuristic is used when something is judged to be a member of a group because of a similarity to the group. This was illustrated by Kahneman and Tversky (1973) when they asked participants to judge the occupation of someone based on a description. The participants were told the description was chosen at random from a set of a hundred descriptions of either lawyers or engineers, half the participants were told there were descriptions of seventy lawyers and thirty engineers and other half told thirty lawyers and seventy engineers. The description given to the participants was like that of a typical engineer but not a lawyer. Participants judged that there was a 90 per cent chance that the person was an engineer no matter what else they had been told, which meant that the decision was influenced by the similarity of the description to an engineer alone.

The second heuristic described by Tversky and Kahneman (1973) is the availability heuristic. They suggest that some judgements of the probability of an event, or that something will have certain characteristics, are based on the availability of information from memory. If people can think of a number of examples they tend to overestimate the probability, but if they cannot think of examples they tend to underestimate probability. Participants were asked whether letters such as K or R were more common as the first letter or as a third letter in English words. Most participants estimate that the letters are more common as the initial letter of words, but really they are both more common as the third letter. Tversky and Kahneman believe that the availability heuristic explains the error because it is easier to think of examples of words beginning with K or R than examples when they are the third letters.

The third heuristic proposed by Tversky and Kahneman (1974) is the anchoring and adjustment heuristic. They suggested that when making estimates or judging probability people often take on initial value, which they called an anchor, and they adjust it. However, most participants do not adjust the anchor much and if the anchor is inaccurate the final estimate or judgement will be inaccurate. If the anchor is very high people will adjust down, but only a little; if the anchor is very low people adjust up, but again only a little bit. For example Tversky and Kahneman (1974) gave participants a random number between 0 and 100 and then asked them if that figure was higher or lower than the percentage of African countries in the United Nations. They then asked the participants to give an estimate of the percentage of African countries in the United Nations. When given an initial figure of ten, participants gave an average estimate of about 30 per cent but if the initial figure was sixty-five the average estimate was 45 per cent. They seemed to use the initial figure as an anchor. Some psychologists have said that the anchor and adjustment heuristic by Tversky and Kahneman can be applied to a variety of real situations such as risk assessment and estimates of property values.

Kahneman and Tversky's approach has been very influential in the study of decision-making. Overall decision-making is part of our everyday life and there are many ideas about decision-making. The heuristics and biases approach introduced by Kahneman and Tversky has dominated the study of judgement and decision-making. Their theory has been used to explain a number of different types of research findings.

Examiner's comment

This answer addresses the question well and it is clear that the candidate has a good knowledge of the topic. However, the answer would only be likely to gain 14 marks (9 for description and 5 for evaluation) because, although it has some very good descriptions of Kahneman and Tversky's work there is very little evaluation or assessment of their explanations.

The first two paragraphs introduce the topic well and clearly identify the explanations of decision-making that are to be discussed. The third paragraph shows that the candidate has a good understanding of the representiveness heuristic, but is almost all description. Only the last two sentences offer any evaluation or commentary on this explanation of decision-making. The next paragraph contains a good description of the availability heuristic, but again only the last sentence offers any commentary on the idea. Unfortunately this pattern is repeated yet again in the paragraph dealing with the anchoring and adjustment heuristic.

The last paragraph does start to evaluate the contribution of Kahneman and Tversky and highlights the positive aspects of their approach. However, the first three sentences all tend to make the same point. There is no mention of the alternative approaches to decision-making that are emerging.

KEY RESEARCH SUMMARIES

Article 1

Hunt, E. and Agnoli, F. (1991) The Whorfian hypothesis: a cognitive psychological perspective. *Psychological Review*, 98, 377–389.

Aim

There had been little interest in the Whorfian hypothesis, that language determines or influences thought, for some years preceding this article. There was little evidence for the strong version and, according to Hunt and Agnoli, the weak version was vague and untestable. This summary will concentrate on the ideas and evidence for the cognitive version of the LRH rather than on a review of the strong and weak versions of the LRH (see pp.10–21 for a discussion of the strong and weak versions). The aim of the article was to present a cognitive version of the linguistic relativity (Whorfian) hypothesis which could be quantified and therefore evaluated. Their hypothesis was that the language a person uses influences the ease (or computational cost) of thinking about particular concepts. Hunt and Agnoli claim (p.379):

> People consider the costs of computation when they reason about a topic. The language that they use will partly determine these costs. In this sense, language does influence cognition.

Method

This is a review article that draws together theories and empirical studies of thought and language to support their thesis. The methodologies of the studies were primarily experimental, but Hunt and Agnoli drew on evidence from cross-cultural comparisons, field observations and what they termed 'thought experiments'.

Evidence

Hunt and Agnoli looked at the influence of language on three aspects of language: lexical effects (i.e. effects of information about words), utterance-level effects (i.e. effects of semantics and syntax) and higher-level effects (i.e. influence of language on reasoning and pragmatics). Lexical effects are the type originally studied by Whorf and Sapir and concentrate on the influence of having more or less words for something in one language that another. Hunt and Agnoli conclude that, although studies show that perception is relatively immune to influences of language, memory is not. They point out that a number of studies of eyewitness testimony show that introducing verbal information can alter recall and recognition. They suggest that a useful source of evidence for the LRH would be to study any effects caused by different levels of ambiguity in words in different languages. For example, differences in the time it takes to comprehend a sentence containing an ambiguous word in one language but not in another. In the discussion of the utterance-level effects Hunt and Agnoli look at the influence of semantics and syntax. They point out that there are differences in the way users of different languages construct sentences and that these have an influence on both comprehension and reasoning. Hunt and Agnoli refer both to the lexical effects and to utterance-level effects as being low-level effects that affect the mechanics of language and suggest that the LRH should be considered primarily by focusing on higher-level effects. The higher-level effects are those linked to the interpretation of the world around us and involve schemas and pragmatics. For example, we develop schemas for dealing with numbers but in some languages the counting system cannot be used for some mathematical concepts such as division. Hunt and Agnoli point to the comparison between the terms used for numbers in English and Chinese. In English there are more terms used to refer to numbers than in Chinese. For example, in English there are thirteen terms to learn between 0 and 12 and then seven 'teen' terms. In contrast, in Chinese there are only eleven basic terms from 0 to 10 because all subsequent terms are a combination of the basic terms (so 11 is '10 and 1' – not a new term). Evidence suggests that English-speaking children have problems learning to count in the teen range but that Chinese children do not. Thus language seems to influence the development of schema about number. Hunt and Agnoli note similar examples of the influence of language on spatial and social schema.

Discussion

Hunt and Agnoli claim that evidence from a variety of sources does suggest that language influences thought. They suggest that this influence should be viewed from a cognitive standpoint and that different languages impose different costs on some types of thought. If a particular way of thinking is more 'costly' in one language compared to another then it is less likely to occur, or may be slower. Hunt and Agnoli (p.387) conclude: 'our review has convinced us that different languages pose different challenges for cognition and provide differential support to cognition'. They acknowledge that the examples they used were selective but suggest they have identified the basis for further empirical research.

Article 2

Saxton, M. (1997) The contrast theory of negative input. *Journal of Child Language*, 24, 139–161.

Aim

This study is concerned with the effect of feedback on language acquisition. Saxton points out that there is an assumption (particularly amongst nativists – see p.57) that parents do not correct grammatical errors in children. However, he believes that the role of negative input has been ignored. He suggests that negative input is any corrective adult response following a child's utterance that indicates the child has made error/s. The contrast theory concentrates on the immediate contrast between the child and adult version and suggests that it is this feedback that provides the information for language acquisition. The aim of this study was to compare the effects of negative versus positive input on the learning of the past tense of a number of irregular verbs. The essential difference between negative and positive input is that negative input is given as a response to an incorrect child version whereas positive is given as a model. Saxton (p.151) illustrates the difference between negative and positive input using the novel verb 'pell', which has an irregular past tense of 'pold':

Negative input
   Adult: What happened?
   Child: He PELLED him on the leg.
   Adult: Yes, he POLD him.
Positive input
   Adult: Look what happened! He POLD him on the leg.

The hypothesis was that children would be more likely to reproduce correct irregular forms of verbs following negative rather than positive input.

Method

This was an experimental design that used thirty-six children with a mean age of 5 as participants. The children were taught six novel verbs with irregular past tense, each of which had been modelled on a real verb. For example, the novel verb 'neak' was used to mean a clapping motion that trapped a target between the palms of the hands. This was modelled on the verb 'speak', so the past tense of 'neak' was 'noke' (i.e. equivalent of 'spoke'). The use of novel irregular verbs ensured that the children were not influenced by prior learning. The experiment used a repeated measure design and each child was given positive input for three verbs and negative for three. The study was counterbalanced and each novel verb was given positive and negative for different participants. After training with either negative or positive input the children's use of the novel verbs was monitored and allocated into categories, including Use Correct (UC) and Persist-with-Error (PE) which broadly correspond to correct and incorrect use of the verb.

Results

The results of the study showed that the percentage of UC responses following positive input was 0 (or in other words there was *no* correct use of the novel irregular verb), but there was 29.6 per cent UC following negative input. There was also a striking difference in the percentages of PE responses (essentially incorrect responses). Following positive input there was 85.2 per cent PE responses, but following negative input there was only 30.6 per cent PE responses.

Discussion

This study suggests that children respond to immediate negative input and are more likely to produce the correct form than when given positive input. Furthermore, children are less likely to reproduce the incorrect form following negative input than positive input. The results of this experimental study are reflected in naturalistic data which show children are more likely to use correct adult language when they are given negative rather than positive input (e.g. Farrar, 1992). Saxton believes that negative input is effective because of the immediate contrast between the child's version and the correct adult version (hence 'contrast theory'). Saxton acknowledges that one limitation of the study is that it is only concerned with the short-term effects of negative input. It is therefore possible that the differences between negative and positive input do not have the long-term effects that would be needed for language acquisition. However, he believes that his experimental approach to the study of language acquisition could be adapted to study long-term effects.

Articles 3 and 4

Kahneman, D. and Tversky, A (1996) On the reality of cognitive illusions. *Psychological Review*, **103, 582–591.**

Gigerenzer, G. (1996) On narrow norms and vague heuristics: a reply to Kahneman and Tversky (1996). *Psychological Review*, **103, 592–596.**

Background

Since the early 1970s Kahneman and Tversky's *heuristics and biases* approach has dominated the field of judgement and decision-making. The concepts they outlined have generated a great deal of research and formed the central core of most of the work in this area. However, since 1991 the approach has come in for some sustained criticism from Gigerenzer and his colleagues. These two articles set out the two opposing views in this intense debate. In the first, Kahneman and Tversky defended their approach in response to the criticisms that Gigerenzer had levelled against it; in the second, Gigerenzer responded. The arguments are complex and detailed and this summary will therefore concentrate on the main points only.

Kahneman and Tversky

The aim of this article was to examine 'the validity of Gigerenzer's critique of heuristics and biases research' (p.583). Kahneman and Tversky suggest that this critique consists of a disagreement about the concept of 'bias' and an empirical claim that errors in judgement can be made to disappear by phrasing the questions using frequencies rather than probabilities or by emphasising that the sampling in the examples is random. The conceptual difference centres on whether the outcome of single events can be described as a probability or not. Kahneman and Tversky believe that it can, whereas they characterise Gigerenzer's position as that of a 'frequentist' who argues that it cannot. If the outcome of single events cannot be expressed as a probability then judgements cannot be biased, hence Gigerenzer's assertion that 'biases are not biases'. Kahneman and Tversky also claim that Gigerenzer's description of their work as being based on narrow norms is incorrect and assert 'contrary to this description, the normative standards to which we have compared intuitive judgements have been eclectic and often objective' (p.583).

Kahneman and Tversky then go on to examine three types of bias which Gigerenzer claims 'disappear' with simple manipulations: base-rate neglect, conjunction errors and overconfidence. After detailed analysis of each they conclude that he has overstated his case and that a more accurate description is that 'some cognitive illusions (not all) are sometimes reduced (not made to disappear) in judgements of frequency' (p.589). They go on to point out that people do make subjective judgements of probability about single events and it is these judgements that guide their actions. Therefore studies based on frequency estimates (which Gigerenzer advocates) are 'unlikely to illuminate the processes that underlie such judgements'.

Gigerenzer

In his reply Gigerenzer argues that the difference between the two positions is largely one of research strategy. He believes that Kahneman and Tversky's heuristics and biases approach has failed to explain the cognitive processes involved in judgements and for two main reasons: they use a narrow view of norms and the heuristics they describe are too vague to be useful.

Gigerenzer suggests that one fundamental difference between his position and that of Kahneman and Tversky is the statistical reasoning. Gigerenzer argues that the laws of probability do not apply to the outcome of singular events but only in 'well-defined circumstances'. However, Kahneman and Tversky use laws of probability to statements about single events and use them in comparison with participant's judgements. Gigerenzer believes this leads to Kahneman and Tversky imposing narrow norms and when participants deviate from these the results are interpreted as cognitive illusions.

Gigerenzer claims that the second main problem of the heuristics and biases approach is that the concept of heuristics is vague and does not explain processes involved. He claims 'the problem with these heuristics is that they at once explain too little and too much. Too little because we do not know when these heuristics work and how: too much, because, post hoc, one of them can be fitted to almost any experimental result' (p.592). In other words, the heuristics do not really explain the findings but act as a description of them.

Gigerenzer believes that, rather than using vague heuristics, 'we will need models that make surprising (and falsifiable) predictions and that reveal the mental processes that explain both valid and invalid judgement' (p.595).

The outcome of the dispute between the two positions is likely to set the direction for future research in this area. This summary has only touched on some of the detailed arguments in both articles and perhaps it is best to conclude with quotes from the postscripts to each article. Kahneman and Tversky suggest: 'we believe that progress is more likely to come by building on the notions of representiveness, availability, and anchoring than by denying their reality' (p.591). Gigerenzer concludes: 'twenty-five years ago ... Kahneman and Tversky opened up a fertile field. Now is the time to plant theories' (p.596).

Glossary

adversarial problems. Problems that involve competing against another person (typically game playing).

algorithms. Problem solving procedures that search all the possible answers to find the correct one.

analogy approach. The heuristic device of adapting solutions to previous problems to solve similar problems.

anchoring and adjustment heuristic. This is the tendency to make judgements about a value by using an initial value (the anchor) and basing the judgement around that value (adjustment).

availability heuristic. The tendency to make judgements based on information available from memory.

babbling. Vowel and consonant sounds ('ga', 'ba') that infants produce during the pre-linguistic phase.

base-rate fallacy. The tendency to ignore base-rate information when judging probability.

child-directed speech. The simplified form of language that adults use when speaking to young children and infants.

conjunction fallacy. The tendency to judge that two events or properties are more likely to occur than either is alone.

connectionist networks. Specialised computer programs that are designed to mimic the way the brain processes information. These programs respond to feedback and are capable of 'learning'.

deep structure. The underlying meaning of a sentence.

echolalia. The repeated production of babbling sounds during the pre-linguistic phase.

egocentric speech. Speech that is not intended to communicate to others but is for the benefit of the speaker.

elaborated code. A form of language that is context-independent and uses complex grammar.

framing effect. The effect of the way a problem is presented on decision-making.

functional fixedness. The tendency to concentrate on the usual function of an object and to neglect other potential uses.

genderlect. The different styles of language used by men and women.

General Problem Solver (GPS). A computer program that uses the heuristic means-ends analysis to solve problems.

goal state. The position a person wishes to achieve when presented with a problem – essentially the solution.

grammar. The system of rules that govern the use of language.

heuristics. 'Rules of thumb' for solving problems or making decisions which act as short cuts but do not guarantee the correct answer.

hindsight bias. The tendency to be more confident about the ability to predict the accuracy of an answer when the correct answer is known.

holophrase. The use of a single word to produce a variety of messages by combining the word with gestures, change of tone and context.

insight. A sudden understanding of the underlying structure of a problem that allows it to be solved.

language acquisition device (LAD). An innate mechanism that allows children to learn a language simply by being exposed to one.

language acquisition socialization system (LASS). The idea that language is acquired because of the need for social communication (i.e. the social equivalent of the LAD).

linguistic relativity hypothesis (LRH) (also known as the Sapir–Whorf hypothesis or the Whorfian hypothesis). This hypothesis is that the language a speaker uses affects the thoughts they have. The strong version is that language determines thought, the weak version that language influences thought.

means-ends analysis. A heuristic device for solving problems in which the problem is broken into stages and an attempt is made to reduce the difference between the start state and goal state at each stage.

non-adversarial problem. A problem in which the person is not in competition with another (typically puzzle solving).

object permanence. The concept that an object exists even though it is out of sight.

one-word stage. The stage of language development when children use single word utterances to communicate; it lasts from approximately 12 to 18 months.

operator. An action that changes the state of a problem.

overconfidence. The tendency to be more confident about the accuracy of a decision than actual performance warrants.

overregularisation (or overgeneralisation). The tendency of children to misapply rules of grammar to irregular forms.

pre-linguistic stage. The stage in language development, lasting from 0 to approximately 12 months, when children do not use language.

problem-solving set. The inflexible and habitual use of a problem-solving strategy.

problem space. The mental representation of a problem.

productive thinking. Thinking in a different way that allows novel solutions to problems.

protocol analysis. The analysis of verbal descriptions (or protocols) of thoughts (or the cognitive processes) when engaged in a task such as problem-solving.

representativeness heuristic. The tendency to make judgements that something belongs to a class or group based on the similarity to a prototype of that class or group.

reproductive thinking. Thinking in familiar ways that involves using previous experience of problem-solving to solve new ones.

restricted code. A form of language that is context-bound that uses relatively simple grammar.

restructuring. A change in the perception or understanding of a problem.

start state. The position a person is in when they are presented with a problem.

structural features. The underlying concepts of a problem that need to be understood to solve it (cf. *surface features*).

surface features. The superficial aspects of a problem that are linked to presentation and are irrelevant to the solution (cf. *structural features*).

surface structure. The words that constitute written or spoken sentences.

syntax. The rules that govern word order and the relationships between words.

telegraphic speech. A type of early speech that uses very short sentences that only contain key words such as nouns and verbs (like a telegram).

transformational grammar. The process which enables the underlying meaning of a sentence (*deep structure*) to be converted to the words in a sentence (*surface structure*).

two-word stage. The stage in language development when children start to combine words to form sentences.

Whorfian hypothesis. See *linguistic relativity hypothesis*.

Solutions to problems

Problems on p.68

1. Nine-dot problem

The answer lies in extending the lines beyond the square made by the nine dots. There is nothing in the instructions that prohibits this, but people tend to impose this restriction.

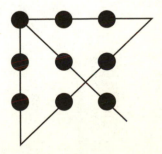

2. Candle problem

The solution is to empty the matchbox and to remove the empty tray and pin it to the wall. The candle can stand in the tray and any wax will collect in it.

3. The water jar problem

The solution is to fill jar B to measure out 42 litres. Then pour out 9 litres into jar A to leave 33 litres. The next step is to pour 6 litres into jar C leaving 27 litres and finally repeat this to leave 21.

Problems on p.72

1. Tower of Hanoi

   i)   Move the small ring to peg C

  ii)   Move the medium ring to peg B

 iii)   Move the small ring to peg B

 iv)   Move the large ring to peg C

  v)   Move the small ring to peg A

 vi)   Move the medium ring to peg C

vii)   Move the large ring to peg C

2. Hobbits and Orcs

The minimum number of crossings that are needed to get the whole party across safely is eleven.

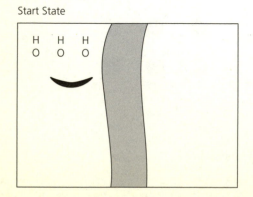

Start State

Move 1.

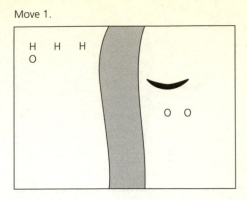

Move 2.

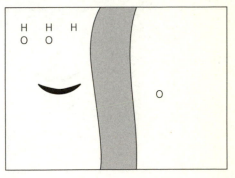

Move 3.

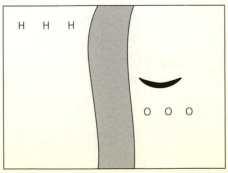

Move 4.

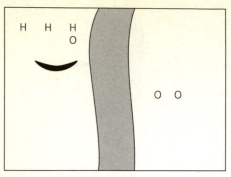

Move 5.

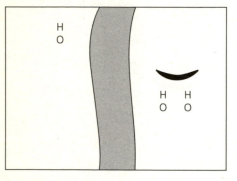

Move 6.

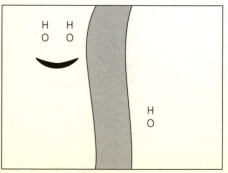

Move 7.

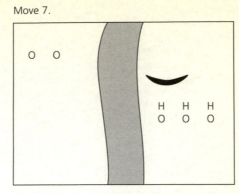

Move 8.

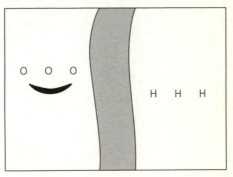

Move 9.

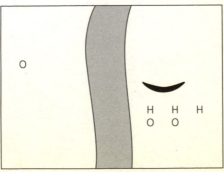

Move 10.

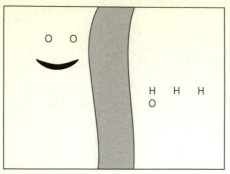

Move 11 = Goal State

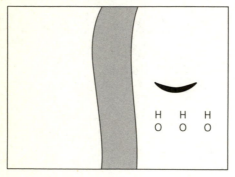

Bibliography

Adger, C. (1997). Dialect education: not only for Oakland. *ERIC/CLL Bulletin*. Washington, DC: ERIC Clearinghouse on Languages and Linguistics.

Bee, H. (2000). *The Developing Child* (9th edn). New York: Longman.

Bellugi, U., Bihrle, A., Jernigan, T., Trauner, D. and Doherty, S. (1991). Neuropsychological, neurological, and neuroanatomical profile of Williams syndrome. *American Journal of Medical Genetics Supplement, 6*, 115–125.

Berko, J. (1958). The child's learning of English morphology. *Word, 14*, 150–177.

Berko Gleason, J. and Greif, E. (1983). Men's speech to young children. In B. Thorne, C. Kramerae and N. Henley (eds) *Language, Gender, and Society*. Rowley, Mass.: Newbury House.

Berlin, B. and Kay, P. (1969). *Basic Colour Terms: Their Universality and Evolution*. Berkeley, Calif.: University of California Press.

Bernstein, B. (1961). Social class and linguistic development. In A.H. Halsey, J. Flaud and C.A. Anderson (eds) *Education, Economy and Society*. London: Collier-Macmillan Ltd.

Bernstein, B. (1971). *Class, Codes and Control*. Volume 1: *Theoretical Studies Towards a Sociology of Language*. London: Routledge & Kegan Paul.

Bernstein, B. (2000). Social class, language and socialization. In

L. Burke, T. Crowley and A. Girvin, *The Routledge Language and Cultural Theory Reader*. London: Routledge.

Blackmore, S.J. and Troscianko, T. (1985). Belief in the paranormal: probability judgements, illusory control, and the 'chance baseline shift'. *British Journal of Psychology*, 81, 455–468.

Bloom, L. (1973). *One Word at a Time: The Use of Single Word Utterances Before Syntax*. The Hague: Mouton.

Bloom, L. (1991). *Language Development from Two to Three*. Cambridge: Cambridge University Press.

Boroditsky, L. (2001). Does language shape thought?: Mandarin and English speakers' conceptions of time. *Cognitive Psychology*, 43, 1–22.

Braine, M.D.S. (1963). The ontogeny of English phrase structure: the first phrase. *Language*, 39, 1–13.

Brown, R. (1973). *A First Language: The Early Stages*. London: George Allen & Unwin.

Brown, R. and Hanlon, C. (1970). Derivational complexity and the order of acquisition in child speech. In J.R. Hayes (ed.) *Cognition and the Development of Language*. New York: John Wiley & Sons.

Brown, R. and Lenneberg, E.H. (1954). A study in language and cognition. *Journal of Abnormal and Clinical Psychology*, 49, 454–462.

Bruner, J. (1983). *Child's Talk*. New York: W.W. Norton.

Burke, L., Crowley, T. and Girvin, A. (2000). *The Routledge Language and Cultural Theory Reader*. London: Routledge.

Cameron, D. (1985). *Feminism & Linguistic Theory*. London: Macmillan.

Cameron, D. (1995). Rethinking language and gender studies: some issues for the 1990s. In S. Mills (ed.) *Language and Gender: Interdisciplinary Perspectives*. Harlow: Longman.

Carmichael, L., Hogan, P. and Walter, A. (1932). An experimental study of the effect of language on the reproduction of visually perceived forms. *Journal of Experimental Psychology*, 15, 1–22.

Carraher, T.N., Carraher, D.W. and Schliemann, A.D. (1985). Mathematics in the streets and in schools. *British Journal of Developmental Psychology*, 3, 21–29.

Carroll, J.B. and Casagrande, J.B. (1958). The function of language classifications in behaviour. In E.E. Maccoby, T.M. Newcombe and

E.L. Hartley (eds) *Readings in Social Psychology* (3rd edn). New York: Holt, Rinehart & Winston.

Carruthers, P. (1996). *Language, Thought and Consciousness: An Essay in Philosophical Psychology.* Cambridge: Cambridge University Press.

Cartwright, J. (2002). *The Determinants of Animal Behaviour.* Hove: Routledge.

Chase, W.G. and Simon, H.A. (1973). Perception in chess. *Cognitive Psychology,* 4, 55–81.

Chomsky, N. (1957). *Syntactic Structures.* The Hague: Mouton.

Chomsky, N. (1959). Review of 'Verbal Behavior' by B.F. Skinner. *Language,* 35, 26–58.

Chomsky, N. (1965). *Aspects of the Theory of Syntax.* Cambridge, Mass.: MIT Press.

Chomsky, N. (1986). *Knowledge of Language.* New York: Praeger.

Chomsky, N. (1995). *The Minimalist Program.* Cambridge, Mass.: MIT Press.

Christian, D. (1997). Vernacular dialects in U.S. schools. *ERIC/CLL Bulletin.* Washington, DC: ERIC Clearinghouse on Languages and Linguistics.

Chronicle, E.P., Ormerod, T.C. and MacGregor, J.N. (2001). When insight just won't come: the failure of visual cues in the nine-dot problem. *The Quarterly Journal of Experimental Psychology,* 54, 903–919.

Clark, H.H. and Clark, E.V. (1977). *Psychology and Language: An Introduction to Psycholinguistics.* New York: Harcourt Brace Jovanovich.

Corrigan, R. (1978). Language development as related to stage 6 object permanence development. *Journal of Child Development,* 5, 173–189.

Curtiss, S. (1977). *Genie: A Psycholinguistic Study of a Modern-day 'Wild Child'.* London: Academic Press.

Davidoff, J., Davies, I. and Robertson, D. (1999a). Colour categories in a stone-age tribe. *Nature,* 398, 203–204.

Davidoff, J., Davies, I. and Robertson, D. (1999b). Colour categories in a stone-age tribe – addendum. *Nature,* 402, 604.

Davies, I.R.L. (1998). A study of colour grouping in three languages: a test of the linguistic relativity hypothesis. *British Journal of Psychology,* 89, 433–452.

Davies, I.R.L. and Corbett, G.G. (1997). A cross-cultural study of colour grouping: evidence for weak linguistic relativity. *British Journal of Psychology,* 88, 493–517.

Davies, I.R.L., Sowden, P.T., Jerrett, D.T., Jerrett, T. and Corbett, G.G. (1998). A cross-cultural study of English and Setswana speakers on a colour triads task: a test of the Sapir–Whorf hypothesis. *British Journal of Psychology,* 89, 1–15.

de Boysson-Bardies, B., Sagart, L. and Durand, C. (1984). Discernible differences in the babbling sounds of infants according to target language. *Journal of Child Language,* 11, 1–15.

DeGroot, A.D. (1965). *Thought and Choice in Chess.* The Hague: Mouton.

Duncker, K. (1945). On problem-solving. *Psychological Monographs,* 58, 1–113.

Eimas, P.D., Siqueland, E.R., Jusczyk, P.W. and Vigorito, J. (1971). Speech perception in infants. *Science,* 171, 303–306.

Eysenck, M.W. and Keane, M.T. (2000). *Cognitive Psychology* (4th edn). Hove: Psychology Press.

Farrar, M.J. (1992). Negative evidence and grammatical morpheme acquisition. *Developmental Psychology,* 28, 90–98.

Fischhoff, B. (1977). Hindsight ≠ foresight: the effect of outcome knowledge on judgement under uncertainty. *Journal of Experimental Psychology: Human Perception and Performance,* 1, 288–299.

Furth, H. (1971). Linguistic deficiency and thinking: research with deaf subjects 1964–69. *Psychological Bulletin,* 75, 58–72.

Garnham, A. and Oakhill, J. (1994). *Thinking and Reasoning.* Oxford: Blackwell.

Gick, M.L. and Holyoak, K.J. (1980). Analogical problem-solving. *Cognitive Psychology,* 12, 306–355.

Gigerenzer, G. (1991). How to make cognitive illusions disappear: beyond 'heuristics and biases'. In W. Stroebe and M. Hewstone (eds) *European Review of Social Psychology* (Vol. 2, pp.83–115). Chichester: Wiley.

Gigerenzer, G. (1993). The bounded rationality of probabilistic mental models. In K.I. Manktelow and D.E. Over (eds) *Rationality: Psychological and Philosophical Perspectives.* London: Routledge.

Gigerenzer, G. (1996). On narrow norms and vague heuristics: a reply to Kahneman and Tversky (1996). *Psychological Review,* 103, 592–596.

Goldin-Meadow, S. and Feldman, H. (1977). The development of a language-like communication without a language model. *Science,* 197, 401–403.

Goodluck, H. (1991). *Language Acquisition: A Linguistic Introduction.* Oxford: Blackwell.

Greene, J. (1975). *Thinking and Language.* London: Methuen.

Greeno, J.G. (1974). Hobbits and Orcs: acquisition of a sequential concept. *Cognitive Psychology,* 6, 270–292.

Gumperz, J.J. and Levinson, S.C. (1996). *Rethinking Linguistic Relativity.* Cambridge: Cambridge University Press.

Haas, A. (1975). The acquisition of genderlect. *Annals of the New York Academy of Sciences,* 327, 101–113.

Haddock, G. (2002). It's easy to like or dislike Tony Blair: accessibility experiences and the favourability of attitude judgements. *British Journal of Psychology,* 93, 257–267.

Harley, T.A. (2001). *The Psychology of Language: From Data to Theory* (2nd edn). Hove: Psychology Press.

Heider, E.R. (1972). Universals in colour naming and memory. *Journal of Experimental Psychology,* 93, 10–20.

Hockett, P.C. (1960). The origins of speech. *Scientific American,* 203, 89–96.

Hoffmann, C., Lau, I. and Johnson, D.R. (1986). The linguistic relativity of person cognition. *Journal of Personality and Social Psychology,* 51, 1097–1105.

Hunt, E. and Agnoli, F. (1991). The Whorfian hypothesis: a cognitive psychological perspective. *Psychological Review,* 98, 377–389.

Johnson, R.D. (1987). Making judgements when information is missing: inferences, biases, and framing effects. *Acta Psychologica,* 66, 109–135.

Kahneman, D. and Tversky, A. (1973). On the psychology of prediction. *Psychological Review,* 80, 237–251.

Kahneman, D. and Tversky, A. (1979). Prospect theory: an analysis of decision under risk. *Econometrica,* 47, 263–291.

Kahneman, D. and Tversky, A. (1982). The simulation heuristic. In D. Kahneman, P. Slovic and A. Tversky (eds) *Judgement Under Uncertainty: Heuristics and Biases.* Cambridge: Cambridge University Press.

Kahneman, D. and Tversky, A. (1996). On the reality of cognitive illusions. *Psychological Review,* 103, 582–591.

Kaplan, C.A. and Simon, H.A. (1990). In search of insight. *Cognitive Psychology*, 22, 374–419.

Knoblich, G., Ohlsson, S. and Raney, G.E. (2001). An eye movement study of insight problem solving. *Memory and Cognition*, 29, 1000–1009.

Kunda, Z. (1999). *Social Cognition: Making Sense of People*. Cambridge, Mass.: MIT Press.

Labov, W. (1970). The logic of non-standard English. In F. Williams (ed.) *Language and Poverty*. Chicago: Markham.

Labov, W. (1972). *Language in the Inner City: Studies in the Black English Vernacular*. Oxford: Blackwell.

Labov, W. (1995). Can reading failure be reversed: a linguistic approach. In V. Gadsden and D. Wagner (eds) *Literacy among African-American Youth: Issues in Learning, Teaching, and Schooling*. Cresskill, N.J.: Hampton.

Labov, W. (2000). The logic of non-standard English. In L. Burke, T. Crowley, and A. Girvin (eds) *The Routledge Language and Cultural Theory Reader*. London: Routledge.

Lakoff, R. (1975). *Language and Women's Place*. New York: Harper Row.

Lenneberg, E.H. (1967). *Biological Foundations of Language*. New York: Wiley.

Lenneberg, E.H. and Roberts, J.M. (1956). *The Language of Experience*. Memoir 13, University of Indiana Publications in Anthropology and Linguistics.

Lichtenstein, S., Fischhoff, B. and Phillips, L.D. (1982). Calibration of probabilities: the state of the art to 1980. In D. Kahneman, P. Slovic and A. Tversky (eds) *Judgement Under Uncertainty: Heuristics and Biases*. Cambridge: Cambridge University Press.

Lieven, E.V.M. (1994). Crosslinguistic and crosscultural aspects of language addressed to children. In C. Gallaway and B.J. Richards (eds) *Input and Interaction in Language Acquisition*. Cambridge: Cambridge University Press.

Loomes, G. and Sugden, R. (1982). Regret theory: an alternative theory of rational choice under uncertainty. *Economic Journal*, 92, 805–824.

Luchins, A.S. (1942). Mechanisation in problem solving. *Psychological Monographs*, 54, 248.

Lund, N. (2002). *Animal Cognition*. Hove: Routledge.

Luria, A.R. and Yudovich, F.I. (1971). *Speech in the Development of Mental Processes in the Child.* Harmondsworth, Middlesex: Penguin.

MacGregor, J.N., Ormerod, T.C. and Chronicle, E.P. (2001). Information-processing and insight: a process model of performance on the nine-dot and related problems. *Journal of Experimental Psychology: Learning, Memory, and Cognition,* 27, 176–201.

MacLeod, C. and Campbell, L. (1992). Memory accessibility and probability judgements: an experimental evaluation of the availability heuristic. *Journal of Personality and Social Psychology,* 63, 890–902.

Maier, N.R.F. (1931). Reasoning in humans: II. The solution of a problem and its appearance in consciousness. *Journal of Comparative Psychology,* 12, 181–194.

Manktelow, K. (1999). *Reasoning and Thinking.* Hove: Psychology Press.

Matlin, M.W. (2002). *Cognition* (5th edn). Orlando, Fla.: Harcourt, Inc.

Maule, A.J. and Hodgkinson, G.P. (2002). Heuristics, biases and strategic decision making. *The Psychologist,* 15, 68–71.

Mayer, R.E. (1992). *Thinking, Problem-solving, Cognition* (2nd edn). New York: W.H. Freeman & Co.

Messer, D.J. (1999). The development of communication and language. In D.J. Messer and S. Millar (eds) *Exploring Developmental Psychology.* London: Arnold.

Messer, D. (2000). State of the art: language acquisition. *The Psychologist,* 13, 138–143.

Metcalfe, J. and Wiebe, D. (1987). Intuition in insight and noninsight problems. *Memory and Cognition,* 15, 238–246.

Miller, G.A. and McNeill, D. (1969). Psycholinguistics. In G. Lindsey and E. Aronson (eds) *The Handbook of Social Psychology, Volume 3.* Reading, Mass.: Addison-Wesley.

Munnich, E., Landau, B. and Dosher, B.A. (2001). Spatial language and spatial representation: a cross-linguistic comparison. *Cognition,* 81, 171–207.

Nelson, K. (1973). Structure and strategy in learning to talk. *Monographs of the Society for Research in Child Development,* 38, 149.

Newell, A. and Simon, H.A. (1972). *Human Problem Solving.* Engleworth Cliffs, N.J.: Prentice-Hall.

Newell, A., Shaw, J.C. and Simon, H. (1963). Chess-playing programs and the problem of complexity. In E.A. Feigenbaum and J. Feldman (eds) *Computers and Thought.* New York: McGraw-Hill.

Owens, R.E. (2001). *Language Development: an introduction (5th edn).* Needham Heights, Mass.: Allyn & Bacon.

Piaget, J. (1950). *The Psychology of Intelligence.* London: Routledge & Kegan Paul.

Piaget, J. (1967). Language and intellectual operations. In H.Furth (ed.) *Piaget and Knowledge.* Englewood Cliffs, N.J.: Prentice-Hall.

Pine, J. and Lieven, E. (1997). Lexically-based learning and early grammatical development. *Journal of Child Language,* 24, 187–219.

Pinker, S. (1994). *The Language Instinct.* Harmondsworth: Allen Lane.

Pye, C. (1986). Quiché Mayan speech to children. *Journal of Child Language,* 13, 85–100.

Robertson, S.I. (2001). *Problem Solving.* Hove: Psychology Press.

Rosch, E. (1973). Natural categories. *Cognitive Psychology,* 4, 328–350.

Sachs, J., Bard, B. and Johnson, M.L. (1981). Language with restricted input: case studies of two hearing children of deaf parents. *Applied Psycholinguistics,* 2, 33–54.

Sapir, E. (1929). The study of language as a science. *Language,* 5, 207–214.

Savage, L.J. (1954). *The Foundations of Statistics.* New York: Wiley.

Savage-Rumbaugh, E.S. and Brakke, K.E. (1996). Animal language: methodological and interpretive issues. In M. Bekoff and D. Jamieson (eds) *Readings in Animal Cognition.* Cambridge, Mass.: MIT Press.

Saxton, M. (1997). The contrast theory of negative input. *Journal of Child Language,* 24, 139–161.

Scheerer, M. (1963). Problem-solving. *Scientific American,* 208, 387–408.

Scollon, R. (1976). *Conversations with a One Year Old.* Honolulu: University of Hawaii Press.

Scribner, S. (1984). Studying working intelligence. In B. Rogoff and J. Lave (eds) *Everyday Cognition: Its Development in Social Context.* Cambridge, Mass.: Harvard University Press.

Shanks, D. (1993). Breaking Chomsky's rules. *New Scientist,* 30 January, 26–30.

Sinclair-de-Zwart, H. (1969). Developmental psycholinguistics. In D. Elkind and J. Flavell (eds) *Handbook of Learning and Cognitive Processes.* Hillsdale, N.Y.: Erlbaum.

Skinner, B.F. (1957). *Verbal Behavior.* New York: Appleton-Century-Croft.

Snow, C.E. (1994). Beginning from baby talk: twenty years of research on input and interaction. In C. Gallaway and B.J. Richards (eds) *Input and Interaction in Language Acquisition.* Cambridge: Cambridge University Press.

Snow, C.E. (1995). Issues in the study of input. In P. Fletcher and B. Macwhinney (eds) *The Handbook of Child Language.* Oxford: Blackwell.

Solso, R.L. (1998). *Cognitive Psychology* (5th edn). Boston: Allyn & Bacon.

Spender, D. (1990). *Man Made Language.* Glasgow: Pandora Press.

Tannen, D. (1990). *You Just Don't Understand: Men and Women in Conversation.* New York: William Morrow.

Tannen, D. (1994). *Gender and Discourse.* New York: Oxford University Press.

Thomas, J.C. (1974). An analysis of behaviour in the Hobbits-Orcs problem. *Cognitive Psychology,* 6, 257–269.

Tomasello, M. (1992). *First Verbs: A Case Study of Early Grammatical Development.* Cambridge: Cambridge University Press.

Tomasello, M. and Farrar, M.J. (1986). Object permanence and relational words: a lexical training study. *Journal of Child Language,* 13, 495–505.

Tversky, A. and Kahneman, D. (1973). Availability: a heuristic for judging frequency and probability. *Cognitive Psychology,* 5, 207–232.

Tversky, A. and Kahneman, D. (1974). Judgements under uncertainty: Heuristics and biases. *Science,* 185, 1124–1131.

Tversky, A. and Kahneman, D. (1981). The framing of decisions and the psychology of choice. *Science,* 211, 453–458.

Tversky, A. and Kahneman, D. (1983). Extensional versus intuitive reasoning: the conjunction fallacy in probability judgement. *Psychological Review,* 90, 293–315.

Tversky, A. and Shafir, E. (1992). The disjunction effect in choice under uncertainty. *Psychological Science,* 3, 305–309.

Von Neumann, J. and Morgenstern, O. (1944). *Theory of Games and Economic Behavior.* Princeton, N.J.: Princeton University Press.

Vygotsky, L. (1962). *Thought and Language.* Cambridge, Mass.: Harvard University Press.

Vygotsky, L. (1972). Thought and language. In P. Adams (ed.) *Language and Thinking.* Harmondsworth: Penguin Education.

Waxman, S.R. and Hall, D.G. (1993). The development of a linkage between count nouns and object categories: evidence from fifteen- to twenty-one-month-old infants. *Child Development,* 64, 1224–1241.

Werker, J.F., Pegg, J.E. and McLeod, P.J. (1994). A cross-language investigation of infant preference for infant-directed communication. *Infant Behaviour and Development,* 17, 323–333.

Wertheimer, M. (1945). *Productive Thinking.* New York: Harper & Row.

Whorf, B.L. (1956). *Language, Thought, and Reality: Selected Writings of Benjamin Lee Whorf.* New York: John Wiley.

Wolfram, W. (1997). Ebonics and linguistic science: clarifying the issues. *ERIC/CLL Bulletin.* Washington, DC: ERIC Clearinghouse on Languages and Linguistics.

Wolfram, W. and Christian, D. (1989). *Dialects and Education: Issues and Answers.* Englewood Cliffs, N.J.: Prentice-Hall.

Wolfram, W., Adger, C.T. and Christian, D. (1999). *Dialects in Schools and Communication.* Mahweh, N.J.: Erlbaum.

Yamanda, J.E. (1990). *Laura: A Case for the Modularity of Language.* Cambridge, Mass.: MIT Press.

Index

Adversarial problems 67, 79–81
African-American Vernacular
   English (AAVE) 32, 33, 36
Algorithms 74, 82
Analogy 77–79
Anchoring and adjustment
   heuristic 91–92, 101,
   108–109
Arbitrariness 2
Asian disease problem 93, 100
Availability heuristic 89–91,
   101; and familiarity 90; and
   recency 90

Babbling 41
Base rate fallacy 87, 101, 115
Behaviour shaping 52, 63
Behaviourism 6
Berinmo 18
Bernstein 30–32, 34, 36
Black English Vernacular
   (BEV) 32, 36

Candle problem 68, 71, 123

Chess 79–80
Child directed speech 54–56,
   62
Chinese 20, 55, 63, 111
Chomsky 10, 53, 57–61, 63
Cognitive psychology 1, 6
Computational cost 19, 110
Conjunction fallacy 87–88, 101,
   115
Connectionist networks 56, 60
Context bound 30, 42
Context independent 31
Contrast theory 55, 112–114
Critical period hypothesis 59

Dani 17
Decision making 4–6, 7,
   85–101, 107–109, 115–117;
   heuristics and bias approach
   86–96; methods of studying
   5–6; theories of 97–100
Deep structure 57
Disjunction effect 99
Displacement 2

Ebonics 32
Echoic responses 53
Echolalia 40
Egocentric speech 22, 25
Elaborated code 30
Ethnic background and language 32–33
Experts 79–81

Feeling-of-knowing (FOK) 76
Framing effect 92–94, 101
Functional fixedness 71

Gambler's fallacy 88
Genderlect 33
Gender and language 33–37;
General Problem Solver (GPS) 74–76, 76, 82
Gestalt approach 69–71, 82
Gigerenzer 96, 101, 114–117
Goal state 66
Government and binding theory 58, 60
Grammar 12, 40, 48, 60; development of 43–44

Heuristics 74, 82–83, 86, 101, 108, 116
Heuristics and bias approach 86–96, 101, 108–109, 115–117
Hindsight bias 95, 101
Hobbit and Orc problem 72–73, 75, 124–128
Holophrases 43, 48
Hopi 12, 14
Hunt and Agnoli 11, 18, 19–21, 110–112

Information processing approach 73–77, 82

Insight 69–71, 76–77
Inuit 12, 14

Judgements 86–96, 97, 99, 101, 107–109, 115–117

Kahneman and Tversky 86–96, 101, 108–109, 114–117
Kiriwina 19

Labov 31, 32, 35, 36
Lakoff 34, 36
Language 1; and ethnic background 32–33; and gender 33–36; and memory 14–16; methods of studying 3–4; nature of 2–3; and perception 16–19; and sexism 35–36; and social class 30–32; and thought 3, 9–27, 105, 110–112
Language acquisition 39–49; theories of 51–63; contrast theory 55, 112–114; environmental theories 51, 52–56, 63; learning theory 52–54; nativist theory 52, 57–61; social interactionist theory 52, 61, 63
Language acquisition device (LAD) 57, 58, 60, 61, 63
Language acquisition socialisation system (LASS) 61
Learning theory 52–53
Linguistic relativity hypothesis, 10–21, 26, 104–106, 110–112; cognitive version 11, 19–21, 110–112; strong version 11, 12–14, 21, 105;

weak version 11, 14–19, 21, 105: weakest version 14–16
Linguistic universals 57

Mands 53
Mean length of utterance (MLU) 4, 43, 44
Meaning 46–47, 48
Means-end analysis 75, 83
Morphology 3, 7
Motherese 54

Nativist theory 57
Navaho 13, 105
Newell and Simon 73–76, 82
Nine dot problem 68, 77, 123
Non-adversarial problems 67, 68–79, 81–83

Object permanence 22
One-word stage 40, 41, 48
Operators 66
Overconfidence 94–95, 101, 111, 115
Overregularisation 44–45, 60

Paradoxes 97
Passive sentences 46
Piaget 10, 22–24, 25, 26, 106
Phonology 2
Pragmatics 3, 7, 46, 47–48, 61, 111
Pre-linguistic stage 40, 48
Principles and parameter theory (PPT) 58
Problem-solving 4–6, 7, 65–83: and analogy 77–79; and everyday life 81–82; Gestalt approach 69–71; information processing approach 73–77;

methods of studying 5–6; types of 66–67
Problem-solving set 71
Problem space 74
Productive thinking 70
Productivity 2
Prospect theory 99–100, 101
Protocol analysis 6, 69

Reinforcement 52, 62
Reproductive thinking 70
Representiveness heuristic 86–88, 101, 108
Restricted code 30–31
Restructuring 69
Risk-taking 86, 93, 100
Russian 17

Sapir 10–11, 104
Sapir-Whorf hypothesis 11
Semantics 3, 7
Semanticity 2
Setswana 17–18
Sexism in language 35–36
Simon (see Newell)
Simulation heuristic 91
Skinner 52–53, 54, 62
Social class and language 30–32
Social interaction theory 52, 61, 63
Spender 36
Standard English 32, 36
Start state 66
Structural features 78
Subjective expected utility theory 97–99, 101
Surface features 78
Surface structure 57
Syntax 3, 7, 17, 63

Tacts 52

Tannen 34, 35, 36
Telegraphic speech 44, 48
Tower of Hanoi 72, 124
Transformational grammar 57
Two-word stage 43
Tversky (see Kahneman)

Vygotsky 24–25, 26

Water jar problem 68, 71, 124
Williams syndrome 23, 106
Whorf 10–11, 12, 13, 14, 26,
    104, 105
Whorfian hypothesis 11
Wug 45

Zuni 16